A PHOTOGRAPHIC HISTORY OF
WORLD WAR II
INCLUDING THE BATTLE OF BRITAIN

A PHOTOGRAPHIC HISTORY OF
WORLD WAR II
INCLUDING THE BATTLE OF BRITAIN

M. Wilkinson

Photographs by the

Daily Mail

Bath · New York · Singapore · Hong Kong · Cologne · Delhi · Melbourne

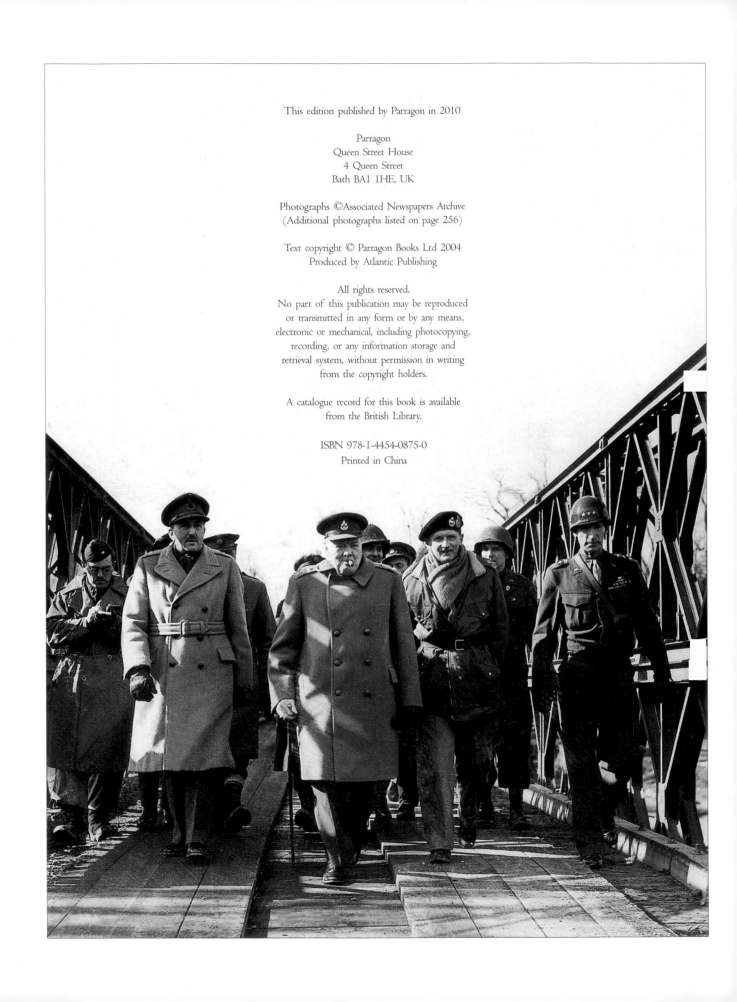

This edition published by Parragon in 2010

Parragon
Queen Street House
4 Queen Street
Bath BAI 1HE, UK

ISBN 978-1-4454-0875-0
Printed in China

Contents

INTRODUCTION 10

CHAPTER ONE THE ROAD TO WAR 12

CHAPTER TWO BRITAIN FIGHTS ALONE 36

CHAPTER THREE A GLOBAL CONFLICT 84

CHAPTER FOUR D-DAY TO PEACE 150

Acknowledgements

The photographs in this book are from the
archives of the Daily Mail.
Particular thanks to Steve Torrington, Dave
Sheppard, Brian Jackson, Alan Pinnock,
Richard Jones and all the staff.

Thanks also to
Maureen Hill, Guy Nettleton,
Cliff Salter, Kate Santon,
Peter Wright and Trevor Bunting.
Design by John Dunne.

WORLD WAR II

A PHOTOGRAPHIC HISTORY

INTRODUCTION

While there had been tension throughout Europe for the best part of the 1930s, few people really believed that the territorially aggressive policies of Hitler's Third Reich would lead to war. With remembrance of the 'Great War' still vivid, it seemed unthinkable to contemplate similar carnage just twenty-one years on from the 'war to end all wars'. The League of Nations and the policy of 'Appeasement', both born out of a desire for humanity to solve problems without resort to bloodshed, seemed to offer ways to prevent armed conflict. Up until the last moment when Germany failed to concede to Britain's demand that she withdraw from Poland, there was a desperate hope that war would be avoided.

When it did come, with the announcement at 11.00 am on 3rd September 1939 from Prime Minister Neville Chamberlain that Britain was 'at war with Germany', it was still a primarily European affair. Hitler had made a non-aggression pact with Stalin's Russia, and the USA, although offering moral and economic support to Britain, did not want to be drawn into what it thought of as the 'Old World's' problems. Nevertheless, by the end of 1941, both these huge countries had been drawn into the fighting, making it a truly global conflict.

World War Two: A Photographic History charts that conflict, from the pre-war tensions to the final reckoning of those guilty of war crimes. The narrative is told principally through photographs, many seen here for the first time, building a comprehensive picture of the lives of people across the globe; lives challenged by fears resulting from dangers, separations, the loss of homes, the loss of loved ones and by the loss of certainties.

The remarkable photographs from the *Daily Mail* archive are restored to original condition, supported and enhanced by an informative text and enlightening captions. These add to the richness of the photographic detail which captures a portrait of a war fought with heroism and sacrifice on every continent.

CHAPTER ONE

The Road to War

In October 1929, panic selling on the New York stock exchange resulted in the Wall Street Crash, which signalled the beginning of the Great Depression. This economic collapse reverberated throughout Europe, and nowhere were its effects felt more deeply than in Germany where the Weimar Republic, established after the First World War, was dependant upon American finance. Unemployment soared and discontent spread. The moderate democratic parties were unable to provide solutions to these problems and people turned increasingly to the extreme parties of the left and right.

THE RISE OF HITLER

The main beneficiary of this disillusionment with democratic parties was the National Socialist (NAZI) Party led by Adolf Hitler, who first came to prominence in 1923 with an abortive attempt to seize power in Bavaria. This 'Munich Putsch' failed, and Hitler was imprisoned. Whilst incarcerated, he wrote *Mein Kampf* (My Struggle), in which he claimed that Germany had not been defeated in 1918 and that the post-war settlement had been a betrayal, for which he blamed the Jews. Following his release in 1924, he reorganised his party and provided it with a private army known as the SA (Sturmabteilungen), which by 1927 numbered over 30,000. These 'Brownshirts' intimidated opponents and provoked violent conflicts with Jews and Communists.

At the beginning of 1930 there were 12 National Socialist members in parliament, but in the autumn elections the Nazis won 107 seats. In 1932 Hitler stood for the presidency and, although defeated, polled over 13 million votes. The parliamentary elections that year saw the Nazis win over 200 seats and become the largest single party. In January of the following year a group of conservative politicians made

a deal with Hitler whereby he became Chancellor. He called new elections for March, and set about ensuring he would gain an overall majority.

On the eve of the elections the parliament building, the Reichstag, was destroyed by a fire which was almost certainly started by the Nazis. Hitler blamed the Communists and used the event to round up his opponents. In the elections he gained a small majority which he used to pass a law giving him power as Chancellor to make laws without the consent of parliament.

With the death in August 1934 of the aged President Hindenburg, Hitler combined the offices of Chancellor and President under the title Fuehrer. The Weimar Republic was no more; Germany was henceforth known as the Third Reich.

FAILURE OF THE LEAGUE OF NATIONS

After the First World War, hopes for world peace had been enshrined in the doctrine of 'Collective Security', and the League of Nations had been established to provide for just such a policy. However, during the 1930s it became obvious that the League was unable to enforce its authority when challenged by a powerful state.

The first challenge had come not in Europe, but in the Far East. Here Japan, a country virtually unknown until 1853, was undergoing an amazing industrial transformation. However, it was a country with limited natural resources, and a rapidly increasing population, which was casting envious eyes on the vast space and potential wealth available in her near neighbour China.

In 1931 Japan attacked and conquered the Chinese province of Manchuria, renaming the state Manchukuo. China appealed to the League of Nations, which branded Japan the aggressor, but took no further action. This weakness was not lost upon aggressors elsewhere and, four years later, the Fascist dictator of Italy, Benito Mussolini, intent on reviving the glorious imperial past of Ancient Rome, launched an attack on the African kingdom of Abyssinia, now known as Ethiopia. The whole apparatus of modern warfare, including heavy artillery, poison gas and air power was launched against the helpless population. Again, the League was powerless and Italy annexed Abyssinia.

SPANISH CIVIL WAR

The League's lack of resolve was further exposed during the bitter civil war in Spain. When the Republican government was attacked by an army led by General Franco, Hitler and Mussolini gave their full support to Franco. Although volunteers flocked to Spain to help the Republicans, Britain and France refused to become involved. Perhaps the most infamous episode was the total destruction of the town of Guernica by German bombers in 1937, seen by many as a precursor to the air raids which were to become

such a feature of the Second World War. In 1939 Franco captured Madrid and became the dictator of another one-party state in Europe. As well as demonstrating the weakness of the democratic states and emphasising the impotence of the League of Nations, the Spanish Civil War had given aggressive Fascist states common cause. At the beginning of November 1936 Hitler and Mussolini signed a treaty which became known as the Rome-Berlin Axis. Later the same month, Japan signed a similar treaty of cooperation with Germany.

LAST CHANCES FOR PEACE

Hitler had already defied the Treaty of Versailles in 1934 when he had begun to rearm Germany, but from 1936 onwards, his escalating demands led inexorably along a path to war. In open defiance of the peace settlement he reoccupied the Rhineland which had been established as a demilitarised zone. German officers on this front were carrying sealed

Below: A group of German officers wearing full military uniform in 1934.

orders which they were to open in the event of their meeting resistance, orders which told them to withdraw. Many commentators feel that this is the last point at which Hitler could have been stopped without war. But, emboldened by the fact that there was no firm response from the League, he now began to build a line of fortifications along the Belgian and French borders. His attention turned next to Austria, which the Treaty of Versailles had decreed should never unite with Germany. In response to disorder plaguing Austria, caused by Austrian Nazis, the German army marched into Vienna and on 13th March 1938 Austria became part of the Third Reich. Hitler returned in triumph to the land of his birth, and to its capital where he had lived in abject poverty before the First World War. His next demand concerned Czechoslovakia, a democratic country created at the Versailles settlement. Within its borders, mainly in the Sudetenland, lived some 3 million Germans whom Hitler insisted should be absorbed into the Reich.

Below: German troops in Berlin swear an oath of allegiance to Adolf Hitler in 1934.

The British Prime Minister, Neville Chamberlain, flew to Germany in September 1938 to discuss these demands with Hitler. At Munich on 29th September it was agreed that the Sudetenland should join Germany. Hitler declared it to be his last territorial demand in Europe, and Chamberlain returned claiming he had secured 'peace for our time'. Critics labelled his policy 'Appeasement'. When Germany occupied the rest of Czechoslovakia and seized the Lithuanian city of

Memel, in March 1939, it was obvious that Hitler could not be trusted and that 'Appeasement' had failed.

COUNTDOWN TO WAR

Domestically, Britain began to accelerate programmes of rearmament and civil defence. On the European stage, the British government suspected that Hitler's next claims would be directed against Poland, and in late March, duly promised to protect Poland from German attack. There was no practical way Britain could help the Poles, but she was confident that fear of Russia would contain German ambitions.

So it was with a sense of shock and foreboding that the world learned that Hitler and Stalin had set aside their ideological differences and mutual loathing, and signed a pact of non-aggression on 23rd August 1939. Secret clauses promised Russia a free hand in the Baltic states and in Eastern Poland. Free from the fear of a war on two fronts, Hitler acted, and on 1st September 1939 Germany invaded Poland. Chamberlain issued an ultimatum, that Germany must withdraw from Poland or face war with Britain. This was ignored by Hitler and when it expired on Sunday 3rd September Britain declared war upon Germany.

Above: A military parade in Berlin, 1935.

'PHONEY WAR'

As Germany took control of Poland, British and French troops maintained defensive positions in Northern France, preparing for the possibility of invasion. However, as the months passed, it seemed increasingly unlikely that Hitler would strike in Western Europe, and talk of a 'phoney war' spread.

The Rise of Hitler

As the leader of the National Socialist Party, Adolf Hitler had led a failed coup against the German government in 1923, resulting in his imprisonment. However, in the ten years from 1924 to 1934, following his release, Hitler was to prey on the fears and disillusionment of the German people, suffering as they were from economic, political and military weakness after the First World War and the continued sanctions placed upon them. Using a combination of propaganda, political manipulation and acts of intimidation perpetrated by his private army, the SA, he was able to secure himself first the position of Chancellor in 1933 and then, following the death of President Hindenburg in 1934, he was to appoint himself Fuehrer. He positioned himself as the leader of a new empire, the Third Reich, and declared his intention to implement a 'New World Order'.

Above: Germany began to prepare for possible attack following the Allied declaration of war. These men are training with the German Air Raid Service in September 1939.

War Declared

On 28th March 1939 Hitler denounced the German pact of non-aggression with Poland, prompting Britain and France to agree to assist Poland in the event of invasion. However, as dawn broke on 1st September, the German Luftwaffe began to strike strategic targets within Poland, with Stuka dive-bombers instilling terror in the civilian population and wiping out the Polish air force in a matter of hours. Simultaneously, nine armoured Panzer Divisions poured across the frontier. Britain's first reaction was to suggest a conference with Germany, but offered an ultimatum when this was met with no response. This expired at 11am on 3rd September and 15 minutes later Britain declared war with Germany, closely supported by France, Australia and New Zealand.

Above: The call up for men was already well underway by the time Britain declared war on Germany; here an official proclamation is read on the steps of the Mansion House.

Left: The British public were quick to support the government's declaration of war against the Nazi regime, and signs such as this one became commonplace.

Opening Moves

The Polish army, consisting mainly of
cavalry divisions such as mounted lancers,
were brushed aside by the German
blitzkrieg or 'lightning war', and by 9th
September the Germans had swept across
the plains and reached Warsaw. On the
17th, Stalin's Red Army invaded from the
east to meet the German forces at the
demarcation line, and by the end of the
month Poland had effectively ceased to
exist. The Polish government and those
troops that were able to do so, withdrew to
Romania, many of them later making their
way to Britain where they would join the
British forces and fight with great
distinction throughout the war.

Right: An expectant
crowd assembles at
Downing Street to hear
the declaration of war.
Many of those gathered
were Czech and German
refugees.

Right: Even prior to the
declaration of war,
children began to be
evacuated from areas
most at risk of
bombing. Schoolchildren
such as these in
Edgware (*right*) were
ferried by bus to railway
stations.

Above: Children greeted by a train driver as they await evacuation.

Evacuating the Cities

As the most likely targets of German bombing raids, London and other major British industrial cities began to see the mass evacuation of schoolchildren to rural areas from September 1939. For many children it would be the first time they had been separated from their families, and would certainly be the first time that most would spend Christmas in unfamiliar surroundings.

Left: A young evacuee headed for Yorkshire says goodbye to her mother and baby sister who remain in London.

Below: A group of children wave goodbye to their families as they wait to board a train.

Opposite: Two youngsters on their way from London to Devon.

Braced for Attack

Whilst Poland was still under attack, British troops began to land in France, but the Allies were unable to mobilise quickly and efficiently enough to be able to prevent the fall of Poland and were expecting instead to fight a defensive campaign. There was little activity in the west as the Germans remained behind their Siegfried Line and the French watched from the Maginot Line, with most of the British forces being concentrated on the Belgian border. Meanwhile, at home, Britain braced herself against a possible attack on the mainland.

Above: Sandbags being filled in Hampstead.

Right: Concrete obstructions such as these were positioned in some open areas to prevent the landing of enemy aircraft.

Above: Troops marching through London soon after Britain entered the war. Some provision for the possibility of war had been made since the early 1930s, but following the handover of the Sudetenland to Germany in 1938, even prior to Hitler's subsequent invasions of Czechoslovakia and Poland, programmes of rearmament and civil defence had been rapidly stepped up.

Left: Part of the preparations for the impending air raids on London involved the protection of various statues and other monuments. Here, Eros in Piccadilly Circus can be seen boarded up, having been first surrounded by sandbags.

Marching to War

Following the declaration of war there was an immediate need to extend the numbers of men in the armed services. In addition to regular soldiers, members of Territorial reserve forces, volunteers and those who were conscripted prepared to be called up to serve as required. A Conscription Bill had been passed in May 1939, and soon afterwards all young men under 21 were registered. The following year, some 30,000 more were signed up.

Above: Civilians report for training at military bases.

The Altmark Incident

Although both the Allied and German forces were initially reluctant to make an offensive move on land, at sea it was a different story. On the 4th September the British liner *Athenia* was sunk by a German U-boat, and a further ten ships would be lost in the first week of British involvement, prompting Chamberlain to restore Churchill to the post of First Lord of the Admiralty, an office he had held 25 years previously. The German Battleship *Graf Spee* had claimed a number of British vessels in 1939, the prisoners from which were then transported on a supply ship, the *Altmark*. In early 1940, contravening international law as the *Altmark* was in neutral Norwegian waters, the ship was intercepted by the British destroyer *Cossack*, boarded, and the prisoners rescued.

Above and Left: The RAF played its part in the *Altmark* incident by locating and identifying the ship. These pilots study maps of the area before embarking on reconnaissance missions.

Right: As the war progressed, the age for conscription would be widened to include men aged up to 50. In 1941 the call up was also extended to single women between the ages of 20 and 30. Most conscripted men were sent into the army and by June 1941 over two million were in the service.

Leaving Loved Ones

Left: Throughout the war uniformed servicemen would become a common sight in Britain, whether they were waiting to be shipped to foreign fronts, home on leave or permanently stationed here, as many RAF crews were. However, this private, George Pinnock of the Highland Light Infantry, was granted just 72 hours leave from his regiment in order to marry his fiancée, Miss Joan Cox, and he would see her just once more before the war was over.

Opposite: The war brought dramatic changes to the lives of women, who were replacing men in all kinds of essential industries, including the munitions factories. In January, Churchill encouraged women to take up such jobs. The picture opposite was used to promote the call – a woman works on making a shell casing at a factory in Southern England.

Like Churchill, the Minister for Labour Ernest Bevin
appealed for women to join the workforce and the
auxiliary services, and in May a Labour Authorisation Law
was passed which meant that almost anyone could be
made to work if required. Women took on many menial
tasks, but they also undertook a great deal of skilled
work, although they were paid at the rate of semi-skilled
workers. Despite this discrimination, they were able to
enjoy a level of independence and respect that had
previously been denied to them. The woman (*above*) is
working as a rubbish collector. Many became part of the
'Land Army', working in agriculture, such as the woman
(*opposite*) driving a tractor.

Digging for Victory

The importance of working the land and growing more crops became increasingly clear with the arrival of rationing in 1940, and many people became involved in agriculture. Allotments were to prove highly popular, and large areas of land were designated for the purpose, eventually with millions of people using them. In March 1940 a special 'Dig for Victory' day was instigated to encourage the public to get involved. Below, people are pictured working an allotment in London's Victoria Park.

Above: Bacon, butter and sugar were the first products to be rationed, quickly followed by other foodstuffs and household goods. More than once during the war attacks on merchant shipping would bring Britain dangerously close to running out of essential supplies.

Left: The trellis-work of tape on this shop window was designed to minimise flying glass in the event of a nearby explosion.

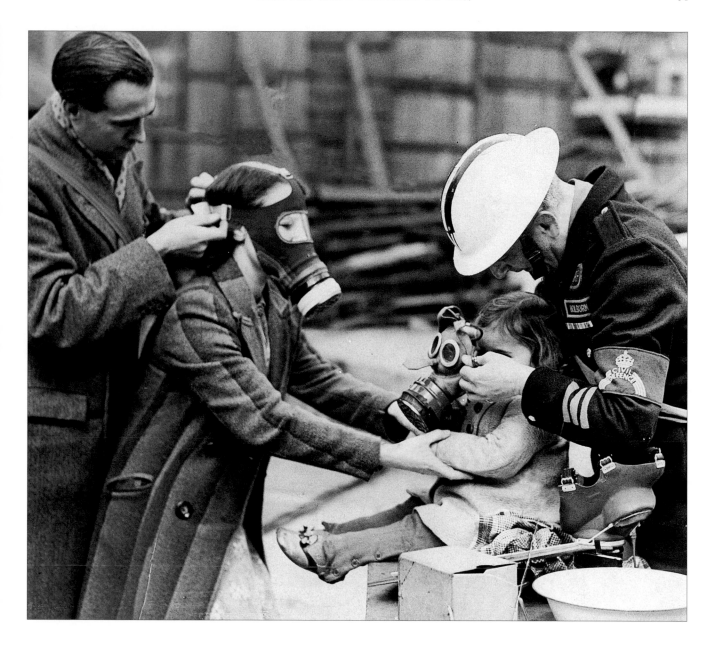

Above: Some 38 million gas masks had been issued in the lead up to war, and came in a variety of sizes and styles to ensure that everyone could be protected in the event of a poison gas attack. It was made an offence not to be in possession of a mask.

Hitler's Threat

In Britain measures were put into effect to combat the expected onslaught from the sky: gas masks were issued, people dug shelters in their gardens and blacked out light from their homes. Places of public entertainment were closed, large gatherings were outlawed and rationing began early in 1940. As a harsh winter progressed, though, people began to wonder if such hardships were necessary and whether Hitler's ambitions might not be confined to Eastern Europe. However, an awareness remained that the rapid fall of Poland meant that German troops could be quickly redeployed for an attack in the west.

Recycling for the War Effort

Iron railings were removed from many public places such as parks, gardens and squares in order to be resmelted for use in munitions, and private owners were encouraged to do the same. There were however some objections, notably from several Lords, and usually in defence of 'historically important' railings. Some were preserved, but most of London's parks and squares were stripped of theirs, and it was a similar story in many cities across Britain. These railings are being removed in Manchester.

Left: The civilian war effort was stepped up, with increased productivity in all kinds of industries. Non-essential goods and services were reduced whilst recycling of various materials, particularly paper and metal, to be used mainly in the manufacture of munitions was increased. Here, a pair of Boy Scouts collect waste paper.

Below: Children in Croydon are encouraged to help in the recycling effort, receiving donkey rides in return for collecting paper.

Observing the Blackout

As the largest city in Britain and the seat of political power, London would undoubtedly be the prime target of any German attack, but other large industrial centres such as Birmingham, Liverpool and Manchester were just as aware of the need to defend themselves. Like London, these cities and others also made provision for air raids, constructing public shelters and observing blackout conditions at night.

Above: This shop in Manchester has taped up its windows and is in the process of constructing an air raid shelter.

Right: Shop displays continued to be lit at night, but they were noticeably dimmer.

Opposite: A view of the Houses of Parliament seen through barbed-wire defences.

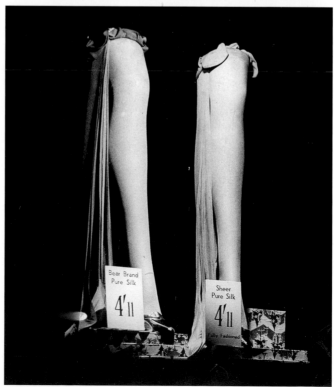

CHAPTER TWO

Britain Fights Alone

Just as the idea of a 'phoney war' was becoming quite widespread, Germany attacked. Firstly, on the 9th April 1940, Hitler's forces launched simultaneous attacks against ports in Denmark and Norway. Contingents from Britain and her Allies already in Norway were rapidly deployed to protect these harbours. Despite strong naval support, lack of reinforcements meant the troops were quickly forced to withdraw by German air power. This withdrawal was spurred on by an even more serious threat to the Allies, for as dawn broke on the 10th May, blitzkrieg was launched against the Low Countries, with German bombardments and paratroopers striking at positions in Holland, Belgium and Luxembourg, facilitating rapid infantry assaults deep into these countries. In response, the Allies committed a large part of their forces to Belgium.

OPERATION DYNAMO

As the German forces advanced through the Low Countries, forcing the Allies towards the coast, armoured Panzer divisions broke through the French lines at Sedan on the 14th May and rapidly ploughed their way across France, heading north towards the Channel coast within a matter of days. At the end of May, as the Low Countries fell into German hands, the Allied forces, caught in a pincer movement, began to retreat towards Dunkirk, where a huge evacuation was to take place. The evacuation was the first test of strength for Winston Churchill who had replaced Neville Chamberlain as Prime Minister on 10th May; Chamberlain had resigned following severe criticism over his handling of the response to the German blitzkrieg in Norway and Denmark.

In an operation codenamed Dynamo, over 330,000 Allied troops were rescued from the beaches of Dunkirk between the 26th May and the 4th June,

utilising whatever boats were available from the English South Coast. Whilst this represented a success in terms of lives saved, thousands of vehicles, weapons and tons of supplies were lost, and Hitler had succeeded in seizing control of the Channel coast.

HITLER SECURES MAINLAND EUROPE

Germany now turned its attention to the rest of France, and in particular to capturing Paris, which fell some ten days later, only one month after the initial attacks in France. In early June Italy entered the war in support of Hitler, and by the 22nd, with Northern France occupied by German troops and columns advancing south towards the Spanish border, the French Premier, Marshal Pétain, had agreed to an armistice whereby France would disarm and be divided into two sections, with a collaborationist government of Nazi sympathisers put in place in the south of the country, based at Vichy.

By the end of the month the Channel Islands had also fallen to Germany, and with most of Western Europe under Hitler's control, he now set his sights on the invasion of Britain, a plan codenamed Operation Sea Lion. For this to be successful, however, dominance in the Channel and on the South Coast had to be established, with Germany launching naval and aerial attacks, first on Allied shipping convoys, and then by August, on the airfields of southern England. The 'Battle of Britain' had begun.

AIR WAR

Although heavily outnumbered by the German Luftwaffe and initially suffering heavy losses, with the advantage of ground radar the Royal Air Force began to regain control of the skies over Britain in late August. The Germans then began to strike predominantly against the urban factories and dockyards

Above: Amongst the most outstanding RAF pilots during the Battle of Britain was James 'Ginger' Lacey, who shot down more German planes than any other pilot, with a total of eighteen.

of London, marking the beginning of the Blitz.

Since the onset of war, Britain had been prepared for the aerial bombardment of such targets, with provision made for air raids, including blackout conditions at night, air-raid shelters, and the mass issue of gas masks, fearing that Hitler would deploy chemical weapons. Although poison gas was never used, casualties were to prove high as densely populated areas were relentlessly bombed. Tragically these casualties included many of those children who had been evacuated to the countryside in the initial months of the conflict, and who had begun to return to their families during the period referred to as the 'phoney war'. However, the Blitz provided some opportunity for the RAF to regroup, and as the Luftwaffe continued to lose many more aircraft than the British forces, the invasion of Britain was called off in September. Bombing raids against industrial cities were to be extended more widely across Britain and to persist for the next two years, but even by September the RAF had begun to retaliate, running bombing missions against German cities.

A WIDENING CONFLICT

Meanwhile, a campaign was beginning to open up in North Africa. In such a highly industrialised and motorised conflict as WWII, the importance of oil could not be underestimated, and a battle was to ensue for the Suez Canal and the oil fields of the Middle East. Italian forces invaded British Somaliland in August 1940, initially forcing a retreat, but Britain began to amass a large force of tanks in the area, and when Italy staged an invasion of Egypt from Libya in September, British and Commonwealth forces rapidly forced them back to Benghazi, whilst Abyssinia, occupied by Italy in 1935, was also liberated. In October, an Italian invasion of Greece was repulsed by the Greeks with the aid of British troops.

So, by the end of the 1940, although Britain had avoided invasion, it faced a perilous future. New fronts had opened as the war spread through the Balkans and in Africa, where vital oil supplies were under threat; with most of Europe under German control Britain, apart from small pockets of resistance, stood almost alone.

Churchill Becomes Prime Minister

From 1937, when Neville Chamberlain became the Prime Minister
of Britain, he was somewhat understandably committed to avoiding
war, preferring to negotiate at all times. However, in his concessions
to Hitler, such as turning a blind eye to German rearmament, the
occupation of the Rhineland and Austria, and in particular by
agreeing to Hitler's claims to the Sudetenland in Czechoslovakia in
1938, Chamberlain had no doubt contributed to the likelihood of
war. He had seemed convinced that Hitler would make no further
territorial demands, but following the German invasions of the rest
of Czechoslovakia, Poland, and then Norway and Denmark in April
1940, he had little choice but to resign. He was replaced by the
more vociferous Winston Churchill, who formed a coalition
government and set about formulating a plan of action.

Below: The Parliamentary
Home Guard is inspected
by Winston Churchill.

Above: German
paratroopers,
May 1940.

Germany Invades the Low Countries

On 10th May 1940, the same day that Winston
Churchill took up office as British Prime Minister,
Germany launched blitzkrieg or 'lightning war'
against Holland, Belgium, Luxembourg and France,
striking hard and fast with bombing, airborne troops,
infantry and armoured units. Holland fell after four
days, whilst Belgium held out only until the end of
the month before its king, Leopold, agreed to
surrender. Allied troops, most of which were
committed to Belgium, were rapidly forced back into
France and a sense of panic ensued as the Low
Countries quickly fell and German divisions swept
across France, threatening to cut off Allied troops in
a pincer movement. The British, and many French,
troops retreated towards Dunkirk in northern France.

Dunkirk

On 21st May the British Expeditionary Force, who were being pushed back across France, counter-attacked at Arras, south of Dunkirk, but they were unable to hold out against the Panzer Divisions. They risked being cut off by others which had circumvented them via Amiens and Abbeville and were taking control of Channel ports such as Boulogne and Calais. Dunkirk appeared to be the only viable point from which to evacuate the troops by sea, and British, French and some Belgian soldiers began to amass on the beaches there. The tanks pursuing them held off for long enough for the Allies to be able to strengthen their defences on the ground, but the beaches were to come under attack from the Luftwaffe throughout the evacuation, which began on 26th May. Three days later, the operation, codenamed Dynamo, was announced to the British public, and a number of civilian vessels became involved in the rescue. By 4th June, almost 40,000 troops had been ferried to the English South Coast from Dunkirk, with still more being rescued from other parts of the coastline. In terms of lives saved the mission was a resounding success and it would allow the Allied troops to fight another day, but Britain had been forced to abandon much of its equipment, as well as control of the Channel coast.

Top: Columns of Allied soldiers await evacuation at Dunkirk.

Below: One of the many ships involved in the evacuation at Dunkirk sets off for Britain. The plumes of smoke beyond are testimony to the constant bombardment endured by the Allied forces throughout the operation.

Above: Towards the end of summer 1940 the first German aircraft began to reach British shores. A flaming barrage balloon plummets earthwards near Dover Castle, having been shot down by a German plane.

Italy Invades North Africa

As the Battle of Britain raged in the skies over the
South Coast, Mussolini widened the offensive by
launching a campaign in North Africa. Following an
unsuccessful foray into British Somaliland in August, on
the same day – 13th September – that Hitler was to
abandon Operation Sea Lion, Italian forces were to begin
an attack on Egypt from their colony of Libya,
penetrating over 50 miles into Egypt, reaching Sidi
Barrani by the 16th where the Italian advance halted.
There was to be no action until December, when
General Wavell launched the first British offensive against
the Italian forces on the 9th. Sidi Barrani was recaptured
the following day, and by the end of the month British
and Commonwealth troops had forced the Italians to
retreat, driving them well back into Libya.

Above: A roll call
for some Egyptian
fighter pilots.

Above: Maltese soldiers of the Royal Artillery, who have volunteered for service in Egypt, practice running to their gun emplacements.

Left: Egyptian guards maintain defensive positions at strategic points such as bridges.

Civil Defence

Even after war had been declared there had been
some doubts that Britain itself would ever come
under attack, particularly during the period known as
the 'phoney war', but following the evacuation of
Dunkirk, attack seemed imminent, and Churchill gave
a rousing speech of unity and defiance. As
continental Europe fell into the hands of the Nazis,
cutting off Britain from her close allies, the
expectation of the invasion of 'Our Island Fortress'
grew considerably, especially in London.

Above: Members of the
Local Defence Volunteers
on parade. Many were
former servicemen who
had seen action in the
First World War.

Provisions for air raids were becoming more organised, with increased numbers of both public and private air-raid shelters, and more effective planning on the part of police, fire crews and air-raid wardens. However, the British population continued to feel the threat of German invasion, precautions for which included the removal of signposts and street names that might otherwise assist invading troops. In addition, various civilian defence groups were formed, united under the title of the Local Defence Volunteers, before being renamed as the Home Guard during the summer of 1940.

The Battle of Britain

Having secured much of Western Europe, Hitler's next move was the planned invasion of Britain, codenamed Operation Sea Lion. In order for such a plan to succeed, however, it was imperative that the German forces first weaken Britain's ability to defend itself by striking at the Royal Air Force. Herman Goering was Commander-in-Chief of the Luftwaffe and he amassed some 3,000 planes along the coasts of Holland, Belgium and Northern France. The first bombing raids were to be directed at British shipping in the Channel, but the Luftwaffe was soon to attack strategic targets on the South Coast such as harbours, factories and airfields. This was to lead to a series of dramatic dogfights over southern Britain as war was waged for control of the skies.

Right and below: Vapour trails of fighter aircraft engaged in aerial combat.

Above: The wreckage of a German plane lies in a farmer's field having been shot down in a dogfight. The pilot survived the crash and was immediately captured.

Left: Although the south-east was most heavily targeted by the Luftwaffe, fighter patrols engaged German aircraft all over Britain. This reconnaissance plane was brought down in Scotland.

Above: Winston Churchill visits Ramsgate, one of the most heavily bombed areas of Britain during the Battle of Britain in 1940.

RAF Outnumbered

Although aircraft production was accelerated, initially the RAF was severely outnumbered, with only around 1,000 fighter planes and a similar number of experienced pilots. However, they were to inflict heavy losses on the Luftwaffe throughout August. The British had the advantages of radar and the fact that the German planes were limited by range, being able to remain airborne for around only an hour and a half before returning to refuel.

Above: A row of British Spitfire fighter planes prepare for take-off.

Left: British airfields were in a constant state of readiness for German attack. These pilots run to their planes to assist in a dogfight which is already under way in the skies above.

The role of RAF fighter pilots and anti-aircraft
gunners was invaluable in protecting Britain from
more severe bombing, limiting damage to towns and
cities whilst enabling the further production of
aircraft to continue. There were periods, particularly
in July and August, when it seemed that the losses of
both men and machines would preclude victory, but
the dedication of a small number of men based in
South East England was to win through and
ultimately prevent German invasion.

Above: British
airmen, hard at
work between
missions, preparing
ground for an
airbase.

Above: A shell is loaded into an anti-aircraft, or ack-ack, gun. These weapons played an important part in defending British airfields and other important installations.

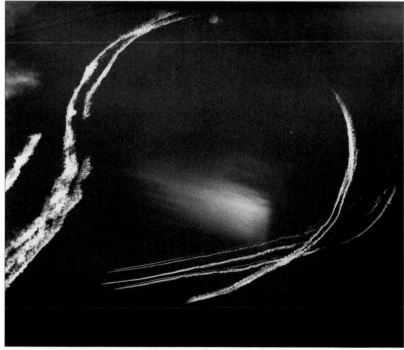

Right: A formation of Spitfires dives into battle leaving trails of vapour.

Above: A squadron of
Hurricane fighters flies
in close formation.
Along with the Spitfire
this aircraft was the best
defence Britain had
against the Luftwaffe.

Left: The wreckage of a
German plane engulfed
in flames, shot down as
it headed home after a
bombing raid.

Above: Two barrage balloons
are downed by German
fighter planes. Barrage
defences were raised as enemy
planes approached in order
to deter low-flying bombers.

Above: German
bombers attacking
over Britain.

Right: Following Italy's
declaration of war on Britain
on 10th June 1940, anti-Italian
sentiment grew in Britain
during the summer, and in
some cases resulted in attacks
on Italians and their property,
particularly their businesses.
This man attempts to protect
his shop with the message that
his company is British.

Right: Whilst anti-aircraft gunners, such as these Bren gunners, kept a watchful eye on the skies over Britain, many civilians played an important role as roof spotters, providing early warnings to the public and to colleagues at factories, other workplaces and institutions.

Below: A group learn to identify aircraft and distinguish between Allied and enemy planes.

Spitfire Production

Right: A Spitfire production line. Whilst the Hurricane was more numerous, and accounted for more German losses than the Spitfire, the speed and agility of the Spitfire made it a formidable fighter plane.

The Few

Britain was losing far fewer planes than Germany, but by the end of August numbers were dangerously low. It was at this time that the RAF was to receive something of a reprieve, for the Luftwaffe now turned its attention to bombing London and provincial cities. However, this change of tactic by Germany enabled the RAF to recover somewhat and throughout the Blitz the Luftwaffe continued to sustain severe losses. As a result, by mid-September Hitler had decided to postpone the invasion. With regard to the British pilots, Churchill announced: 'Never in the field of human conflict was so much owed by so many to so few'.

Left: Squadron Leader Douglas Bader was one of the most remarkable RAF pilots of the Battle of Britain, having lost both of his legs in a crash in 1931. His artificial limbs proved no hindrance, and he was regarded as a particularly skilful pilot.

Above: Bader, having just received the DSO pictured with Pilot Officer W.L. Knight (right) and Flight Lieutenant G.E. Ball.

Right: Members of the Women's Auxiliary Air Force (WAAF) in training. Although women did not fly combat missions, the contribution of women in the auxiliary services was invaluable. The WAAF staffed radar stations whilst, amongst other duties, the women in the ATS manned anti-aircraft guns, and those of the Air Transport Auxiliary flew missions delivering new aircraft.

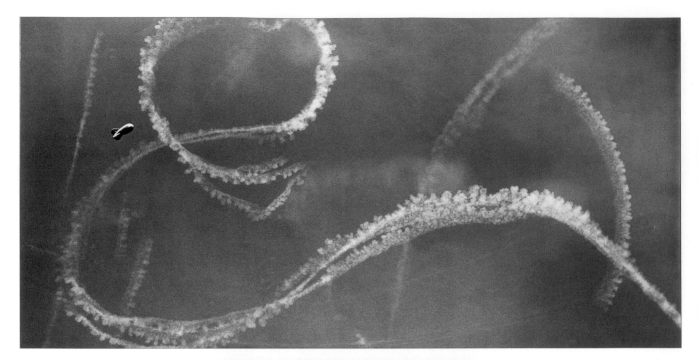

Above and Right: Daytime dogfights marked by vapour trails as British fighters engage the Luftwaffe during the Blitz.

Industrial Targets

Despite the blackout, barrage defences, anti-aircraft guns and the best efforts of Britain's RAF fighter pilots, London and other cities suffered considerable damage during the Blitz. Following the losses sustained during the Battle of Britain, the Luftwaffe attacked mainly at night, making defence more difficult. The targets were mainly industrial, such as dockyards and factories, but in such densely populated areas, air raids inevitably resulted in the destruction of civilian property and loss of life.

Above: A row of taxis
destroyed by bombing in
London's Leicester Square.

Surviving the Blitz

The Blitz created some frightening and difficult times for Londoners, but generally it seemed that the public attempted to continue with life as normally as possible and the attitude was one of defiance, courage and unity in the face of adverse conditions. To some small extent this was bolstered by propaganda, but the Blitz undoubtedly fostered a very real community spirit.

Above: Civilians shelter during an overnight air raid in the relative safety of Holborn Underground station. Although there had been initially been some objections to the use of Tube stations as air-raid shelters, their benefits were obvious, and the train system continued to function despite the extra crowds.

Above: Seemingly undeterred, these workers bombed out of their office building continue their jobs in the street, protected only by their steel helmets.

A Classless War

Before the war, social divisions in Britain were
deeply marked, and although this remained the
case in 1941, the war was beginning to bring
people closer together. Public air-raid shelters
became something of a leveller, places where
different classes could mix with each other, and
the middle classes, who enjoyed a far higher
standard of living, began to become more aware
of the poor housing conditions and high
unemployment endured by a large proportion of
the working classes.

Opposite: Even the ruling
classes were not unaffected
by the air raids on
London. Following a night
of heavy bombing during
which Buckingham Palace
suffered damage, the
Queen speaks with families
in London's East End.

London Hit

The first bombs dropped upon London at the beginning of what would later become known as the Blitz were targeted at the docks and industrial areas of London's East End in daylight. It was only a matter of days before the carnage was spread across the city and the bombs began falling at night. Until May 1941, when the air raids became far less frequent, London and many other major British cities were frequently and heavily bombed, leaving some areas close to ruins.

London's Regent Street (*above*) and Bruton Street (*opposite*) badly damaged following a night of heavy bombing.

London's stations thronged with soldiers during the war, as did much of the capital, and as the years passed, the build up of troops in Britain increased dramatically. Soldiers from Eastern Europe, France, and later Canada and the USA, joined the streams of British troops departing for and returning from fronts in Europe and beyond.

Right: A British soldier, heavily laden with equipment, pauses for a mug of tea at a London station.

St. Paul's Survives the Blitz

Above: Although St. Paul's Cathedral was bombed during the war, including being hit by a bomb which lodged in the foundations without exploding, it remained relatively intact. On the night of Sunday 29th December, hundreds of incendiary bombs were dropped on the City of London sparking massive fires which severely damaged many of the surrounding buildings. The cathedral survived unscathed and this photograph of the event was to become one of the most enduring and iconic images of the Blitz.

Above: Women and children
queue for food at a
communal cooking centre
set up by the London
Council.

Right: A temporary Post
Office during trials in
London. It was designed to
be portable and could be
erected swiftly in order to
replace Post Offices which
had been damaged by
bombing.

Above: Urban bombing destroyed hundreds of homes and businesses, leaving many civilians homeless and shops and services wiped out. However, people had little choice but to adjust to these challenging circumstances and most did so well. Provisions were made for the homeless, with buildings such as schools being used as temporary accomodation.

Above: Firemen train their hoses on the
John Lewis department store in London's
Oxford Street. It was completely gutted by
fire after bombing on the night of 18th
September 1940.

Palace Damage

Opposite: The King, Queen and Prime Minister
Winston Churchill inspect wreckage at Buckingham
Palace. This was one of several occasions upon
which the palace was damaged during air raids. The
Royal Family remained in residence throughout the
war, however, a fact that for many Londoners
bolstered a sense of solidarity.

Battle of the Dover Straits

Whilst the Blitz raged on the mainland, shipping, which had been targeted almost immediately after Britain's declaration of war on Germany, continued to brave bombardment from the Luftwaffe whilst also suffering the constant threat of mines and U-boat attacks. Following the fall of France, the Germans also trained long range guns on the South Coast and employed them against shipping. The convoys were vital in bringing food and other supplies into Britain, and the naval campaign which raged in the English Channel and the Atlantic was to prove the longest of the war.

Below and Right: German attacks on Allied shipping in the Channel.

Above: An Allied
merchant ship is guided
through a minefield by
means of semaphore.

Devastating Raids Nationwide

Above: Although London was perhaps the most heavily and regularly bombed British city, others such as Coventry, Birmingham, Manchester, Liverpool, Bristol and Southampton also suffered from devastating air raids. On 14th November, Coventry city centre was almost completely destroyed by fires started by night-time bombing.

Right: A few days after the bombing King George visited the city with the Minister for Home Security, Herbert Morrison.

Above: Just over a week after the attack on Coventry, Birmingham was bombed relentlessly in an attack which lasted some eleven hours. The following morning, firemen continue to deal with a blaze at a Birmingham factory.

Bombing Germany

Although no full air offensive was launched
upon Germany in the first two years of
conflict, several bombing raids were made
against German cities in retaliation for
attacks on Britain.

Right: A Berlin street
following an RAF raid
in retaliation for heavy
bombing in London
the previous week.

Below: Members of the
German Safety Service
tackle a blaze caused by
incendiary bombs
dropped on Berlin.

Above: Berliners gather to survey bomb damage in a central street.

Berlin Blitzed

Following the devastating and somewhat demoralising attacks rained down on Britain by the Luftwaffe, particularly after the assault on Coventry, the desire was certainly present amongst the British people, Bomber Command and the government to put Germany under similar pressure. To that end, the RAF stepped up its air raids against Berlin.

Right, below and opposite: Bomb damage is cleared away from homes and shops in Berlin, destroyed by British air raids.

Above: Families sheltering at Piccadilly Circus Underground station during an air raid. The London Underground provided a haven for many Londoners, though some concerns were raised about a small minority of people who became too frightened to return above ground and adopted a subterranean existence throughout much of the Blitz.

Princess Elizabeth's First Broadcast

Princess Elizabeth made her first broadcast in 1940. It was a task that her father hated, due to a stammer, so the BBC used to record his voice in small sections at a time. Elizabeth, however, embraced the challenge and would record her speeches live.

CHAPTER THREE

A Global Conflict

As the winter of 1940 passed into 1941 the Blitz against London and other British cities continued and intensified. On 16th and 19th April, German attacks killed more than a thousand people on each night in London, and 148,000 homes were damaged.

BATTLE OF THE ATLANTIC

At sea, the Battle of the Atlantic raged, as convoys of supplies vital to British survival faced constant attack from U-boats and Luftwaffe bombers, which were by now operating from bases along the coastline of a conquered France. America was the main source of these supplies for Britain, but the cost was beginning to prove crippling to Britain's wartime economy. Despite the USA's reluctance to become involved in what it saw as a European affair, President Roosevelt was willing to give any support short of military involvement. So, in response to an appeal from Churchill in March 1941, the American President persuaded Congress to pass the Lend-Lease Act, which allowed America to lend war materials to a country whose defence was perceived as necessary for the safety of the USA. This enabled British resistance to continue. Relationships between the two countries were strengthened further when, in August, Churchill and Roosevelt met and issued the 'Atlantic Charter', in which they stated their reasons for resisting aggression.

MEDITERRANEAN EXPANSION

Mussolini's interventions in North Africa on behalf of his German ally had proved singularly unsuccessful in 1940 but, in the spring of 1941, the picture changed dramatically as Hitler intervened in support of the Italians. Romania, Hungary and Bulgaria had by now been forced to join the Axis and, in April, a devastating attack was launched against Yugoslavia and Greece. British troops were evacuated to Crete, but the island and its garrison fell to German paratroopers in May.

Meanwhile, in North Africa, one of the greatest generals of the war was about to make his mark. By the end of April the Afrika Korps, under the command of General Erwin Rommel, had driven the British out of Libya, back across Egypt to within range of the Suez Canal. In November, however, the British advanced once more, relieving Tobruk in early December.

OPENING OF THE RUSSIAN FRONT

Perhaps an even more decisive moment came on Sunday 22nd June, when, reneging on the Moscow-Berlin Pact of 1939, Germany launched its invasion of Russia, codenamed 'Operation Barbarossa'. Churchill pledged immediate support for Russia, and during the summer the Americans agreed to extend their policy of Lend-Lease.

Initially the Russians retreated, taking with them anything that might be of use to the invaders, and operating a 'scorched earth' policy, whereby any supplies that could not be taken with them were destroyed, as were bridges, railways and fields of crops. By September, Leningrad was surrounded by German troops. Kiev fell in October and by the end of November the Germans had reached the outskirts of Moscow. However, Russia was well equipped to defend Leningrad and Moscow, and at the end of the year a counter-attack was launched against the Germans, who were now faced with the problem of surviving the bitter Russian winter.

JAPANESE ATTACK PEARL HARBOR

As the Russians were launching their attack, the war became a truly global conflict when, on Sunday 7th December 1941, a force of Japanese planes launched from aircraft carriers attacked the American naval base at Pearl Harbor in Hawaii. The attack came without warning and was to prove devastating to the forces based there, wiping out almost all of the planes and boats, and killing over 3,000 troops. The following day, America declared war on Japan, as did Britain and its allies.

British naval power in the Pacific suffered a crippling blow when two of its largest battleships, the *Prince of Wales* and the *Repulse*, were sunk by Japanese bombers on 10th December. Conflict in the Pacific escalated rapidly as Japan made several lightning strikes throughout the region, and by the end of the year the American bases at Guam and Wake Island had fallen. Hong Kong was captured on Christmas Day, and attacks were launched on Burma and Malaya.

Enigma Machine Captured

Earlier in the year, however, the Allied forces had had some dramatic successes in the Atlantic. On 7th May, a German weather ship, which was captured off Iceland, was found to be carrying secret documents concerning the German coding machine, Enigma. Two days later, in a piece of good fortune, a captured U-boat was found in possession of a cipher machine and code books. This enabled British code-breakers, based at Bletchley Park, to eventually break the codes used to issue orders to the submarine fleet.

Later the same month the German battleship *Bismarck* sailed from the Baltic to the Atlantic on a mission to attack the vital Atlantic convoys. On 24th May as she passed the Denmark Strait, she was intercepted by Britain's greatest battleship HMS *Hood*. In the ensuing action, the *Hood* sustained a series of direct hits and sank within minutes, with the loss of 1,415 men. Only three of the crew survived.

Once in the Atlantic, however, the *Bismarck* was pursued by British warships and ancient, torpedo-carrying Swordfish planes. With her steering mechanism disabled by repeated attacks, the ship was located on 27th May by a group of British warships comprising HMS *Rodney*, *King George V*, *Norfolk* and *Dorsetshire*. In the battle which followed, the *Bismarck* was sunk and the greatest surface threat to the Atlantic Convoys was removed.

Pacific Battlegrounds

Following the attack on Pearl Harbor and victories in Malaya, Hong Kong, Thailand and the Philippines in December 1941, Japanese forces moved swiftly in an attempt to seize control of South East Asia, launching attacks throughout the Pacific that would put Allied forces in the region under immense pressure. In January 1942, Manila, the Dutch East Indies, Kuala Lumpur and Burma were invaded. By February British troops in Malaya were forced to retreat to Singapore, which fell on the 15th, with some 80,000 British and Australian personnel being captured. Later that

The Japanese attack on Pearl Harbor wiped out almost all of the planes and boats, killing over 3,000 troops.

month Japan attacked Australia, bombing Darwin. On the 26th the Japanese were to land on Java, having defeated British and Dutch naval forces in the Battle of the Java Sea. By early spring it seemed that the Japanese were irrepressible, forcing British troops to withdraw across the mainland from Burma towards the Indian border, and capturing islands throughout the eastern Pacific.

SIEGE OF STALINGRAD

In Russia, the Red Army had held out over the winter, and had some success in pushing the Germans back from Moscow in January, but by May the German Army had regrouped and was ready to launch a new campaign in the area. The plan was to attack the Crimea in the south, prior to seizing control of the Caucasus which held vital supplies of oil. Initially the Germans were quite successful, capturing Rostov and Sevastopol in June and July. However, turning north in August in a push towards Stalingrad, the German advance was slowed by Russian resistance and finally checked in the suburbs of Stalingrad itself.

The besieged city was to be desperately defended and, as winter set in, the Russians launched a counter-offensive, inflicting heavy casualties. They surrounded the Germans to both the north and south of the city. Trapped, the German forces of the Sixth Army and the Fourth Panzer Division awaited resupply and the arrival of a relieving army, but by December any such attempts were an evident failure.

ALLIED SUCCESS AT EL ALAMEIN

In North Africa, 1942 was to begin with something of a stand-off, as both sides regrouped on either side of the 'Gazala Line'. In May, as the Germans attacked in Russia, Rommel launched his next attack on the British, outflanking them and forcing a rapid withdrawal to Tobruk, which was lost by June. The British Eighth Army retreated eastwards to El Alamein, where they were to receive rapid and vast reinforcement from the Suez Canal area, and were able to successfully hold the 'Alamein Line' despite sustained attacks in July and August. By October, under the command of General Montgomery, the British Army was ready to strike back. On the 23rd, following a huge artillery bombardment, 'Operation Lightfoot' led a frontal assault against Rommel's forces, quickly pushing them back from Egypt into Libya.

With his forces heavily committed to defending Russia, Stalin had hoped that Britain and America might by now be ready to launch an invasion of Western Europe, thus diverting some of Hitler's forces to a new front and relieving pressure on Russia. President Roosevelt agreed with the strategy in principle, but at this stage was advised against pursuing it by his generals. Prime Minister Churchill, however, was even more sceptical, preferring to press on towards regaining a foothold in North Africa and the Mediterranean. On 8th November, under the command of the American General Eisenhower, a large-scale invasion of French North Africa was launched with the codename 'Operation Torch'. The Anglo-American forces met little resistance, with the commander of Vichy France, Admiral Darlan, whose forces were occupying the area, ordering a ceasefire just two days after the invasion began. In response, Hitler scrapped Marshal Pétain's Vichy government and ordered the full occupation of France.

As the Allies began to close in from the west, taking possession of Morocco and Algeria, Montgomery's troops continued to advance from the east, recapturing Tobruk on 13th November and Benghazi around a month later. The Axis troops were to receive some reinforcement from Sicily but, in something approaching a rout, they were now being forced into Tunisia in a pincer movement.

DIEPPE DISASTER

Meanwhile, in something of a concession to the call to open a second front in Western Europe, Churchill authorised what he described as 'a reconnaissance in force to test the enemy defences'. The result was 'Operation Jubilee', a large-scale raid on the French port of Dieppe. On 19th August an Allied force of some 6,000 troops, mainly Canadian but aided by British and Free French Commandos and American Rangers, landed on the beach, supported by the Royal Navy and the RAF.

In military terms the raid was a disaster with thousands of Canadians being killed. After nine hours the force was withdrawn and, of the 6,000 troops who had set out, only 2,500 returned. However, important lessons had been learnt about the problems of attacking in the vicinity of large, heavily defended buildings which would be put to good effect in the eventual invasion of Normandy.

War at Sea

Whilst May had marked the beginnings of campaigns in both Russia and North Africa that were to prove decisive for the Allies by the end of the year, a similar pattern was occurring in the Pacific. The Battle of the Coral Sea took place between 4th and 7th May, when the Japanese invasion fleet bound for Australia was intercepted by American aircraft carriers off New Guinea. Although there were losses on both sides, the Americans effectively negated the potential threat to Australia and the Japanese fleet turned back. Then, almost exactly one month later, the Battle of Midway was to witness the destruction of four Japanese aircraft carriers, severely reducing their capabilities and heralding a shift in fortune for the Allies, who would begin to gain the upper hand in terms of naval and air power in the region. This provided the opportunity for Allied attacks to be launched in the Solomon Islands and the first landings took place at Guadalcanal in August, where fierce fighting was to rage for the rest of 1942. Naval battles were also to continue in the area, and in November the Americans inflicted further heavy damage to the Japanese Navy and to a supply convoy off Guadalcanal.

In the Atlantic, Allied convoys were still under regular attack from German U-boats, warships and disguised merchant vessels. Despite some successes the previous year, including the sinking of the *Bismarck* and the interception of valuable codes, the threat to Allied shipping remained high. Not only were the Allied convoys facing attack as they brought supplies to Britain, but now they carried lend-lease supplies to Russia, bringing convoys perilously close to German-occupied Norway and the surrounding areas, where both air and naval activity were high. Improved radar, sonar, radio intercepts and air cover enabled the destruction of some 87 U-boats in 1942, but there was a marked increase in Allied losses too. In July, the convoy PQ 17 was to lose 22 supply

Right: Although the Luftwaffe raids became less intense after the summer of 1941, German bombing would continue to represent a threat to lives of British civilians throughout the war. Here, an injured police constable removes furniture from the wreckage of his home.

ships, followed in September by a German attack on PQ 18, which resulted in the loss of 13 vessels.

GIs Reach Britain

On the British mainland, a massive programme of airfield construction was underway in East Anglia and from these new bases, the Eighth United States Army Air Force, flying their B17 Fortresses and B24 Liberators, began their daylight bombing raids on German cities. Within weeks of the attack on Pearl Harbor and Hitler's subsequent declaration of war on the USA, American troops had begun landing in Britain, and throughout the year they were to arrive in vast numbers. These GIs (so called because their equipment was stamped 'General Issue') were mostly welcomed in Britain, but there were violent incidents between white and black GIs. These were usually caused by white troops who, being used to the strict segregation that existed at home, were unable to accept that their black colleagues could mix freely and on equal terms with the British population. The GIs proved particularly popular with British women and by the end of the conflict some 20,000 British women would have become 'GI brides'.

Social Changes

The conscription of women had begun in December 1941 and continued throughout 1942 until, by the following year, nine out of ten single women were either serving in the forces or working in war

industries replacing men who were in the forces. They worked in shipyards, munitions factories and in agriculture, with the Women's Land Army eventually comprising some 80,000 'Land Girls'. Despite the realisation that they were making a vital contribution to the war effort they were paid far less than men doing the same work.

However, social reform was a key issue in 1942. The main priority remained defeat of the Axis forces, but British politicians were also considering what sort of society they wished to see when victory was eventually achieved. There was a general feeling that Britain had to become a better place to live in after the war than it had been throughout the twenties and thirties. The way forward was set out in the Beveridge Report: Sir William Beveridge proposed that, after the war, a system of social security for all be set up, with the establishment of a National Health Service and the payment of family allowances. The report became a bestseller.

1943 – A Year of Victories

The triumphs in North Africa in 1942 marked the beginnings of a change in fortune for the Allied forces and were to provide the springboard for a succession of victories in 1943. Montgomery led an advance westward from Egypt through Libya and, by the end of January 1943, he had pushed the Germans back 1,000 miles. Elsewhere in North Africa, General Eisenhower had led an invasion of Morocco and was pushing east. Trapped between these two forces, the position of the Axis armies was hopeless and, in May, following Rommel's escape to Europe, the 275,000-strong German army surrendered to the Allies.

Italian Surrender

The victory in North Africa, and the resulting control of the Mediterranean, opened the way for an attack on Italy. In July, British, American and Canadian troops invaded Sicily, capturing the island within six weeks. This led to the overthrow, capture and imprisonment of Mussolini. By September the Allies had crossed to the mainland and the Italian government surrendered. However, the fighting persisted as the Germans in the country continued to resist and, in an audacious raid, German glider pilots rescued Mussolini from his remote mountain prison. He was flown to Munich before being returned later to Northern Italy.

The Germans now treated Italy as a conquered country and the Allies were forced to fight their way north up the peninsula. Resistance was strong, as at the fortified hill-top monastery of Monte Cassino, where German troops held out against Allied forces for six months.

German Defeat at Stalingrad

Whilst the Germans were being swept out of North Africa, they were also suffering defeat in Russia. Having besieged Stalingrad for several months, successfully infiltrating the city in September 1942, the German army had found itself surrounded by Russian forces since the November. Despite lacking supplies of winter uniforms, food and medicine, and with temperatures reaching 24 degrees below freezing, Hitler refused to allow their surrender. On 31st January, however, following a massive defeat south west of Stalingrad, the German troops, under the command of Field Marshal Paulus, disobeyed Hitler and the German army suffered its greatest ever defeat. Stalingrad marked a major turning point on the Eastern Front. The Russians, bolstered by lend-lease, much of which reached Murmansk through the heroic efforts of the Atlantic convoys, began to push the Germans back westwards.

U-boats Destroyed

1943 also marked a decisive phase in the Battle of the Atlantic. At times Britain's food supplies had been desperately low, as German submarines maintained attacks on Allied merchant ships, but in May 1943, a

Right: An anti-aircraft gun production line.

Above: American Flying Fortress bombers amidst a barrage of anti-aircraft fire during a daylight raid on Berlin, 1944.

famous convoy, codenamed ONS-5, came under attack from the U-boat 'wolf packs'. In the ensuing action, a combination of air attack, gunfire and depth charges from the escort vessels destroyed six submarines. From then on, aided by an increase in American production of vessels, Allied naval power began to gain the upper hand.

THE DESTRUCTION OF HAMBURG

As the Allies began to assert some superiority in the Atlantic, so too they began to carry the war to Germany by air. Throughout the year, the Allies began to bomb targets in the heart of Germany, the RAF by night and the American Air Force by day. Air Marshall Harris had become Chief of RAF Bomber Command in February of the previous year and had begun to plan for a thousand-bomber raid on a single German city. The plan was put into operation on 30th May, when 1,046 bombers took off to attack Cologne. Attacks were made on industrial sites and cities throughout Germany, and in July and August a series of night-time raids by the RAF resulted in the destruction of Hamburg, with the loss of over 40,000 civilian lives. On the night of the 18th–19th November the first mass raid was carried out on Berlin.

THE HOME FRONT

Meanwhile, in Britain life had not returned to normal. Rationing was to continue, as was the build up of foreign Allied troops, especially Americans, Canadians and Poles, but air superiority had led to the end of the full-scale Blitz, and had brought some small relaxation in regulations. Early in the year it was ruled that lights in railway carriages could be left on when trains were standing at stations, and it was later agreed that traffic lights could be used and pedestrians were allowed to carry undimmed torches. However, small-scale bombing raids were still common, particularly over London, usually occurring in retaliation for attacks on German cities. Perhaps the most tragic incident happened on the night of 3rd March during a minor raid in the East of London. People were entering Bethnal Green Tube station to seek shelter when someone lost their footing at the top of the stairs, resulting in a crush in which 178 people lost their lives.

BATTLE IN THE PACIFIC

In the Far East the struggle against the Japanese continued, with the brunt of the fighting in the Pacific being borne by the Americans whilst the British concentrated on Burma. The Japanese had overrun Burma in 1942, and their presence there posed a threat to India. The British launched a counter-offensive but were repulsed in August, after which the Japanese installed a government and declared Burmese independence. In response, the British decided to reorganize their command, and Lord Mountbatten was made Supreme Commander in South East Asia. Perhaps the most colourful British leader in the area, however, was Major General Orde Wingate, whose force of 3,000, known as the Chindits, operated in small columns in the jungle, hundreds of miles behind enemy lines.

The Japanese suffered an earlier blow in April; Admiral Yamomoto was killed when the aircraft in which he was flying was shot down over the Solomon Islands. The Americans then began their fight back in the Pacific, taking most of New Guinea and beginning their policy of 'island-hopping' from the outer ring of Japanese conquests towards Japan itself.

THE GUSTAV LINE

1944 opened with heavy fighting in Italy, where Allied forces attacked the German 'Gustav Line', which crossed the country between Naples and Rome. This attack was reinforced by a surprise landing at Anzio, south of Rome, on 22nd January. In the following month the Germans counter-attacked in this area and Allied advances stalled. However, further heavy attacks in the spring resulted in the Allies breaking the 'Gustav Line' in early May. The Germans were forced from Cassino and Allied troops reached Rome on 4th June.

Desert War

At the start of 1941 Italian forces were pushed back across Libya by British and Australian troops, sustaining major losses at the Battle of Beda Fomm, where hundreds of tanks were captured and around 130,000 Italians were taken prisoner. However, Italy's fortunes changed dramatically as Hitler committed troops to support them. General Erwin Rommel's Afrika Korps arrived in Libya whilst many British troops were being redeployed to Greece in expectation of a German strike there. They immediately began to fight back towards the Suez Canal and the oil fields of the Middle East, forcing the Allies back to Egypt in April. Conflict also occurred in Kenya, Somaliland and in Abyssinia throughout the year, with British and Commonwealth troops fighting alongside Haile Selassie's guerrillas. Abyssinia was reclaimed with the surrender of 20,000 Italian troops in November.

Above: Australian troops in the Libyan desert.

Germany Captures Greece and Crete

At the same time that Hitler came to Mussolini's aid in North Africa, he was also deploying his forces across the Mediterranean in Greece and the Balkans. By now, Hungary, Romania, Turkey and Bulgaria were in German control, having been forced to join the Axis nations. Greece and Yugoslavia were invaded on 6th April. Where the Italian invasion of Greece the previous year had been repulsed by British and Greek troops, the German blitzkreig was again employed to devastating effect and the countries quickly fell. By the end of the month British and Australasian troops had been forced to retreat to Crete, along with two Greek divisions, where they would hold out for a further month. German paratroopers invaded the island on 20th May and there was over a week of heavy fighting before the island was eventually captured. Although many British troops had been evacuated to Egypt, some 18,000 left on Crete were imprisoned.

Top: German paratroopers board transport planes in Greece.

Centre: The paratroopers were deployed with minimal equipment, most of their supplies being dropped separately. Initially this provided a twofold advantage to the Allies, for the Germans were outgunned, and much of their kit was captured.

Bottom: Despite setbacks, the paratroopers were deployed in sufficient number to establish a foothold on the island, and began to battle for overall control.

Lend-Lease and the Atlantic Charter

Just two days after Britain had declared war on Germany in September 1939, President Roosevelt had proclaimed the USA's neutrality. However, two months later he made the concession of selling arms to the Allied forces. Then, in July 1940, with Britain having sustained heavy naval losses, the recently elected Winston Churchill appealed for Roosevelt's help. He responded by supplying 50 destroyers in return for leases on British bases in Newfoundland and the Caribbean. Roosevelt pledged to keep America out of the war, but also believed that the United States should support Britain. Following a further appeal by Churchill in which he requested 'Give us the tools and we'll finish the job', Roosevelt proposed the Lend-Lease Act whereby the US would lend or lease supplies to any nation considered 'vital to the defence of the United States'. Congress passed the Act on 11th March 1941, and the alliance between Britain and the USA was further strengthened in August with the drafting of the so-called Atlantic Charter, which put forward a series of principles for post-war reformation. These were to include the proliferation of democracy, free trade and disarmament, and would later form the basis of the United Nations.

Hand-in-hand with the concept of 'total war', and specifically in a highly industrialised conflict, came the widely held belief that production be dedicated to the war effort, with consumption kept to a minimum. The rationing of food, clothes and other necessities maintained a basic standard of living, whilst all labour and materials were placed under direct state control. With the advent of Lend-Lease from the USA, the speed of production was dramatically accelerated, particularly with regard to vehicles, armaments and ammunition.

Opposite below: Following the First World War the production of armaments had not been a priority, but by 1940 rifles as well as other small arms and equipment were being produced around the clock in British factories.

Opposite above: Production lines turned out shell casings by the thousand.

Above: Production methods were revolutionised in British shipyards by the adoption of American techniques. The aim was to manufacture a battleship each week.

Women and the Workplace

Whilst many workers toiled long hours in armament factories, all kinds of jobs, not necessarily directly related to the war industries, needed to be done. With so many men serving in the forces, women took up a huge variety of positions. Female workers were not merely confined to light duties, as can be seen by these 'Women Navvies' (*right*) shifting heavy stones, but were also involved in demolition and construction work.

Above: A female bricklayer repairing part of a wall damaged by bombing.

Opposite: By September 1941 many women were working full time for the postal service and were provided with a uniform that included trousers, something of a first.

Right: Clothes rationing began on 1st June 1941, and everyone was issued with coupons with which to buy their clothing. Campaigns such as 'Make do and Mend' also encouraged people to repair older garments.

Below: With petrol in short supply, many people took to cycling. With the use of a tandem, this city gent is still chauffeured to work.

The Home Front

Life on the home front continued to throw up challenges and required some getting used to, but the years of austerity and disruption were faced with resolve and a will to pull together to achieve a common goal.

Above: Bus seats being removed to make room for extra standing passengers.

Right: Temporary diversions and evacuations of premises were a further disturbance caused by the German bombing.

Above: With food in short supply, more and more people supplemented their diets by growing their own vegetables, sometimes in unlikely places. Even bombsites were put to good use and converted into allotments.

Opposite: The Land Army mobilised.

Left: RAF bombers striking at low level during a strategic daylight raid against a power station in Cologne.

The Bombing Continues

Although the worst of the Blitz was over by May 1941, air raids continued to bring destruction to British cities. Along with London, industrial cities in the north of England such as Sheffield, Manchester and Liverpool were badly affected, and although not originally intended as a primary target, Hull was relentlessly bombed at the start of May. Referring to the event, Herbert Morrison, the Minister for Home Security, declared: 'Night after night Hull had no peace'. Bombs continued to fall on the city during the summer months and this residential district was devastated in July (*above*).

RAF attacks continued in Germany too, and were widened. Like London, Berlin was the prime target for aerial assaults, but strategic attacks on industry and infrastructure elsewhere were important in maintaining pressure on the German war machine.

The Eastern Front

Over 2,000 aircraft, 3,000 tanks and three million German troops had been amassed on the Russian frontier in June 1941. These were divided into three main groups: Army Groups North, Centre and South. However, Stalin was reluctant to make the first move, seemingly unwilling to believe that Germany would attack. As a result, when the invasion known as Operation Barbarossa began, Russian forces in the border areas were quickly overcome. Smolensk was the first major city to fall to Hitler's troops, being captured in July, with Kiev taken in September. In the same month the siege of Leningrad would begin.

Right: Women help to construct defences around Leningrad as the German forces advance.

Right: As the Russians fell back in the summer of 1941, following a scorched earth policy, they destroyed anything that might be of use to the German armies. Such tactics inevitably slowed the German advance.

Leningrad

By mid-September 1941 Leningrad had been encircled and was being regularly shelled, leaving its inhabitants soon facing the prospect of starvation. In October, however, Britain and the USA pledged a joint declaration of aid and some supplies began to get through.

'Operation Typhoon', the German advance on Moscow, also began in September and by November 1941 German troops were on the outskirts of the city. However, it seemed that Hitler had underestimated the size, strength and resilience of the Red Army, expecting the campaign in Russia to be swift. As the harsh winter set in the German Army found itself poorly equipped to deal with both the extreme cold and the defiant Russian resistance.

Left: A combination of fierce fighting and a scorched earth policy leaves very little for the invading Germans to claim as their own.

Pearl Harbor

Prior to their official entry into the war, the USA had been pushing at the bounds of neutrality. Since 1940, American naval observers had been attached to the Royal Navy, and in 1941 US involvement in the war was stepped up in terms of the provision of supplies to Allied forces. From September, anti-U-boat patrols began off the coast of North America, and military involvement came a step closer when the destroyer *Greer* was attacked by a German submarine. The result was that Roosevelt ordered that any Axis vessels within the American Defence Zone be shot at on sight. Furthermore, in mid-September 1941, US ships began to escort Allied convoys between Newfoundland and Iceland. Despite this, America remained officially neutral. However, this position, and ultimately the course of the war, would change as a result of an attack on the US base at Pearl Harbor by the Japanese in December.

Above: The USS *Arizona* sinks, engulfed in smoke and flames.

Below: The destroyer USS *Shaw.*

As Japan had become increasingly aggressive, diplomatic relations had deteriorated, and had worsened still further in September 1940, when Japan signed a tripartite act with Italy and Germany. In 1941, following Japanese demands for control of French Indochinese colonies, both the USA and Britain had frozen Japanese assets. Negotiations had begun in November, but on 1st December Japan had rejected American terms, prompting Roosevelt to appeal to Emperor Hirohito for peace on 6th December. On the morning of 7th December, with no declaration of war, Japan launched a devastating attack on the American military base at Pearl Harbor on the island of Oahu in the Pacific. The strike took the base completely by surprise and, in under two hours, 18 US vessels, including five battleships, had been sunk. 188 American planes were destroyed, 162 damaged, and 2,403 American lives were lost. A further 1,178 personnel were injured. Japanese losses were minimal by comparison, with the destruction of just 29 planes and the loss of 64 lives. The following day America and Britain were to declare war on Japan.

Above: The huge propeller and part of the hull of the *Arizona*.

Left: A massive cloud of smoke rises after the first wave of attacks, making accurate bombing more difficult. A Japanese plane can just be made out through the smoke.

Battle for the Pacific

The attack on Pearl Harbor, and America's subsequent entry into the war, took the conflict to a truly global scale. The Pacific became a vast arena for several major campaigns. Japanese motivation for entering the war was primarily economic, with the country seeking to take control of resource-rich territories in the area. Following diplomatic breakdown, Japan no doubt hoped that the strike on Pearl Harbor would prevent any rapid American intervention. In this respect the attack was well judged and, in the closing weeks of the year, Japan acted swiftly, launching several devastating attacks. As Britain and the USA declared war on Japan on 8th December, Japanese forces attacked Wake Island, Hong Kong, Thailand and Malaya. Just two days later, Japanese bombers sank both the *Prince of Wales* and the *Repulse*, seriously damaging British naval power in the Pacific. That same day, Japanese troops succeeded in capturing the island of Guam and made landings on Luzon in the Philippines. Wake Island fell on the 23rd and Hong Kong was surrendered to the Japanese on Christmas Day. By the end of the year, Japan had a stranglehold on the region, and Allied forces were struggling to cope.

Above: A line of Japanese battleships with the Mitsu nearest the camera.

Japan Strikes

As 1942 began, the Japanese maintained pressure on Allied forces
in the Pacific and continued to launch attacks throughout the
region, stretching the Allies' ability to respond effectively. In less
than three weeks Manila and Kuala Lumpur had fallen, and
invasions had been launched in the Dutch East Indies and Burma.
On 1st February, British, Indian and Australian troops in Malaya
were forced to retreat along the Malay Peninsula to Singapore.
Outflanked, outgunned, and lacking sufficient air and naval
support, thousands of Allied troops were to surrender on the 15th.
Further north, fighting was to continue for some months but Japan
would eventually triumph here too. The Japanese continued to
strike in multiple locations, taking the islands of New Britain,
New Ireland and the Admiralty Islands, even bombing Darwin on
Australia's north coast on 19th February.

Above: A Japanese
soldier during a
skirmish in Burma.

Battle of the Java Sea

On 26th February Japanese forces gathered to land on the island of Java with heavy naval support. The Allied fleet that sailed to intercept them was hopelessly outnumbered. The ensuing Battle of the Java Sea was to effectively witness the destruction of Allied naval opposition in the South-west Pacific, and the Japanese rapidly overran Java. In early March, Japan invaded New Guinea and captured Rangoon in Burma, and the following month the Allies were evacuated from the country. The Philippines also fell in April, with American and Filipino troops surrendering the Bataan Peninsula on Luzon on the 9th. Some 70,000 Allied prisoners were then forced to march around 70 miles to prison camps in the interior of the country. This became known as the 'Bataan Death March' with around 10,000 prisoners dying due to starvation and maltreatment before reaching their destination. Thousands more would die in Japanese prison camps during the course of the war.

Above: American GIs manning a Howitzer launch in an attack on Japanese troops in Burma.

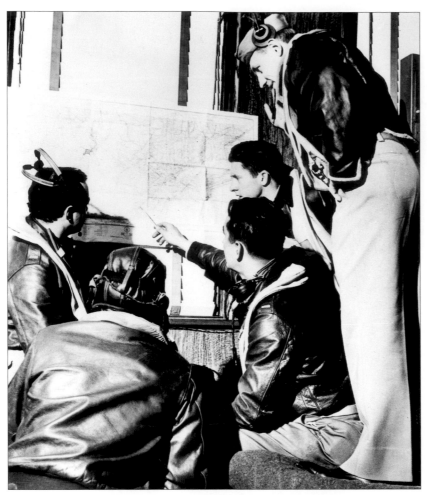

US Military Relocates

Following America's entry into the war, a large part of the American military began to be relocated to Britain, the Pacific and other foreign bases, but there were a number of squadrons that remained based in America. These were responsible for transporting men and materials across the country as well as supporting convoys and defending American shores. From September 1939, the US Air Force had been flying 'Neutrality Patrols' in order to oversee the safety of American shipping in the Atlantic but, following the events at Pearl Harbor, USAF squadrons in America were on high alert, running observation and pursuit missions, and daily Anti-submarine Warfare (ASW) patrols. Bombers were dispatched on more than one occasion in response to coastal attacks by Japanese submarines.

Left and below: Pilots in America were on constant standby in case of an attack on their shores.

Left: Churchill addresses the nation in June 1942. From 18th–25th June he had been in the USA for talks with Roosevelt. Their topics for discussion included the protection of shipping, the diversion of German forces from the Russian front and atomic research.

Below: Americans gather to enrol for the US Air Force in New York.

The Baedeker Raids

From the end of April to early June 1942, the Luftwaffe spread their destruction beyond strategically important industrial centres, targeting picturesque, historic British cities such as Bath, Canterbury, Exeter, Norwich and York. These cities had far fewer air defences than cities such as London and over 50,000 homes were destroyed, killing 1,637 civilians and injuring 1,760 more.

Above: York Guildhall ablaze after an attack on 28th April.

Right: The gutted interior of a church in the city of Bath, hit during raids on 25th and 26th April.

The bombing raids took their name from the German *Baedeker* tourist guide of Britain, from which the targets were reputedly selected. The strikes are widely believed to have originated in response to the Allied bombing of the ancient town of Lubeck in northern Germany, which was being used to supply Nazi troops on the Russian front.

Above: These people were made homeless following a raid on Canterbury in June 1942.

Left: A church in York smoulders following a Luftwaffe raid on the city.

GIs

Just seven weeks after the raid on Pearl Harbor and America's entry into the war, US troops began landing in Britain. They were mostly welcomed, but became somewhat notorious for being 'overpaid, oversexed and over here'. The relationship between the British people and the American troops was complex. A colour bar operated in the US military and many white troops could not accept that their black colleagues mixed freely and on equal terms with the British population. Following several violent incidents between white and black GIs, including shootings, many saw them as trouble-makers. Women also regularly complained about the unwanted advances of American servicemen, but generally the GIs were particularly popular with the female population.

Above: The first contingent of US troops arrives in Britain.

Right: A US Jeep makes for an unusual sight on a London street.

Above: An American
soldier enjoys a Bank
Holiday fair in
Hampstead, 1942.

Right: With the arrival of American GIs in 1942, luxury items such as stockings became easier to obtain, but many women simply pencilled or painted their legs to give the impression of a seam. This woman is using a device designed to give a perfectly straight line.

Below: British and American troops arrive at a British port by train in advance of the Allied invasion of North Africa in November 1942.

The First 1,000 Bomber Raid

In May 1942 Sir Arthur Harris of Bomber Command assembled the largest-ever fleet of bombers, 1,047 in all, to be directed at a single target. Originally intended for Hamburg, Germany's second largest city and a major site of U-boat production, poor weather caused the raid to be switched to Cologne. To gather the desired number of aircraft many inexperienced crews were committed to the attack. There had been some concern about the possible outcome of the mission, but overall the venture proved to be a resounding success. On the night of 30th May, the aircraft flew in a tight stream, maintaining height and speed, both to avoid collisions and to limit German radar detection. The mission was achieved more quickly than had ever been attempted, even for a much smaller force. Although some of the crews missed their intended target, almost 900 planes bombed Cologne, releasing 1,455 tons of bombs, two thirds of which were incendiary devices.

Raid on Dieppe

In 1942 the Allied forces were not yet ready to mount a full-scale invasion of Western Europe, but it was decided to launch a large, though somewhat speculative, raid on the French port of Dieppe. Originally planned for July, the mission was postponed to August due to poor weather and given the codename 'Jubilee'. The attack took place at dawn on 19th August and involved just over 6,000 troops, the majority of whom were Canadian, aided by British and Free French Commandos, and a small group of American Rangers. The troops were supported by eight destroyers and around 70 airborne squadrons. The plan involved landing at five separate positions along the coastline and eliminating resistance on the flanks, before units converged on the town of Dieppe itself, with a frontal assault timed to occur 30 minutes after the initial landings. However, the main attack force was pinned down on the beaches, coming under heavy fire from German positions in sea-front buildings. Although some infantry managed to infiltrate the town, they became engaged in fierce fire-fights, and lacked the back up of tank regiments, which came ashore late and had difficulty negotiating the sea-wall. The supporting air squadrons also suffered heavy losses. By the time the operation was called off in the afternoon it had proven a terrible failure, with the loss or capture of over 3,000 men. Although lessons were learnt that would no doubt ultimately reduce the loss of life on D-Day, the cost of these lessons had been severe.

Above Major General J.H. Roberts (right), commander of the Canadian forces at Dieppe.

Right: Part of the first Hurricane squadron that flew to Dieppe.

Operation Blue

In early 1942, the German offensive in Russia was focused mainly in the south, with Hitler redirecting forces from Army Groups North and Centre to Army Group South in an attempt to seize Stalingrad and to secure the mineral rich lands of the Crimea and Caucasus regions. The German southern campaign, or 'Operation Blue', unfolded relatively slowly in the spring, and although the build up of troops in those areas was certainly worrying, Stalin was reluctant to divert troops from Moscow. As a result, the operation gathered pace in the summer with the ports of Rostov and Sevastopol being captured in June and July. Although the advance was then slowed, by late summer German and Axis forces were poised to attack Stalingrad, reaching the outskirts of the city by August.

Left: Russian marines engage the enemy on the Black Sea coast, July 1942.

Below: New Red Navy torpedo boats set out on a mission in the Black Sea.

Stalingrad – No Retreat, No Surrender

In the first stages of the attack on Stalingrad, the Luftwaffe almost completely reduced the city to rubble, backed up by assaults from Panzer Divisions. Vicious hand-to-hand fighting raged throughout September and October as the Germans advanced. Although the Germans soon controlled almost 90% of the beleaguered city, having lost only around 8,000 troops, compared to an estimated 80,000 Russians, the Red Army maintained their fierce resistance. Whilst the fighting continued Russian General Zhukov formulated a plan of counter-attack; 'Operation Uranus'. The plan was to redirect Russian forces from Moscow to encircle the German flanks of the Sixth Army which were protected by less well-equipped Romanian, Hungarian and Italian troops.

Above: A Russian anti-tank crew on the outskirts of the city.

Red Army Attacks

The operation involved the deployment of over 10,000 heavy guns, almost 1,000 tanks, and over 1,000 aircraft. Having surrounded the Axis forces, the Red Army attacked to the north on 19th November, and to the south two days later, rapidly gaining the advantage. Hitler refused to allow retreat or surrender, instead commanding Field Marshal von Manstein's Don Army group to relieve the trapped Axis armies. However, they were to be repelled on 12th and 13th December, and withdrawn on Christmas Eve.

Left: Armed Russian workers take up defensive positions on the roof of their factory.

Below: Much of Stalingrad was destroyed by shelling and street fighting.

North Africa: El Alamein and Operation Torch

After attacks and counter-attacks in the deserts of North Africa throughout 1942, it was decided to open a second front in the region, with an Allied invasion from the west, landing troops in Morocco and Algeria. A huge Anglo-American invasion force of over 400 ships, 1,000 aircraft and some 107,000 troops was assembled, with some vessels sailing directly from the USA, the longest voyage ever undertaken prior to such a landing. The primary objectives of the invasion were the occupation of Tunisia, in order to prevent the reinforcement and resupply of Axis forces in Libya, and to take pressure off the Allied Eighth Army whilst establishing a pincer movement, closing down on the enemy from the west, as Montgomery's forces advanced from the east.

Up to this point, after conflicts in January and February, the British had been driven back from the German line at El Agheila to Gazala, where a stalemate had ensued. Then on 26th May Rommel had launched a new offensive, rapidly forcing the Allies back to El Alamein in Egypt, dangerously close to the vital Suez Canal. The Allied Eighth Army dug in and prepared for Rommel's assault. It was launched on 1st July, but after three weeks of fighting, German and Italian forces were unable to breach the Allied defences, and in August, with his supply lines overstretched, Rommel began to be driven back. On 23rd October, having by now been heavily reinforced, Montgomery's forces took the offensive, and, following heavy artillery fire, assaulted the Axis lines with infantry and armour. By early November, having lost around 50,000 men, Rommel's forces began to retreat, and by the end of the month had been pushed back to El Agheila.

During the lull in fighting prior to the Battle of El Alamein, conflict had continued in the Mediterranean Sea, as both Axis and Allied warships, submarines and aircraft sought to attack opposing supply convoys. The British colonial island of Malta was to prove invaluable as an Allied base for such operations and was bombed mercilessly by both Italian aircraft and the Luftwaffe. In April alone almost 7,000 tons of bombs were dropped on the island, severely affecting its operational capabilities for some time, but the civilians and troops bravely resisted attack throughout the war and it was never captured. On April 15th 1942 Malta was awarded the George Cross.

Left: Part of the vast armada of ships which sailed to Africa in order to open a new front on the west of the continent. Although protected by accompanying warships, many of the vessels carrying troops were actually ocean liners.

The 'Torch landings', commanded by General Eisenhower, began on 8th November with troops deployed at Safi and Casablanca in Morocco, and on beaches at Algiers and Oran in Algeria. After brief conflicts with French forces Admiral Darlan, commander of Vichy France forces stationed in North Africa, ordered a ceasefire on 11th November, and French cooperation was assured. The Allies now began to close in on the Axis armies from both sides, forcing them into Tunisia.

Left: American troops wade ashore at Arzeu, having been delivered from their ships by landing craft.

The End in Africa

In early February 1943, the Allied Eighth Army was to reach the Tunisian border where Rommel's forces, reinforced by over 100,000 German troops from Sicily, maintained defensive positions along the so-called 'Mareth Line', halting the Allied advance before it could reach the capital, Tunis. Rommel then went on the offensive on 14th February, deploying heavy armour in a bid to break through the Allied lines and seize territory around Tebessa. The Allies were taken by surprise, and hurriedly withdrew, being pushed back around 100 miles, but when this drive was eventually checked towards the end of the month, Rommel pulled his forces back. Two strikes were then launched in early March against the British First and Eighth Armies, but these too were to prove unsuccessful, and gave the Allies the chance to launch a counter-offensive.

Above: Two British soldiers (seated) look on as American troops land near Algiers.

Rommel in Retreat

British and US forces attacked at the 'Mareth line' and the Eighth Army performed an outflanking manoeuvre that by the end of the month had sent Rommel's forces into a major retreat. Rommel himself was called back to Germany just days later. By mid-April the Axis troops were tightly contained in the hills around Bizerta and Tunis and, following heavy fighting, the Allies led a final drive through these areas in early May, with both cities falling between 7th and 11th May. By the 12th, there was no longer any resistance from the Axis armies, and around 275,000 Germans and Italians were to surrender on the Cape Bon Peninsula, ending the campaign in North Africa.

Left: Captured Italians being driven through Algiers to internment camps shortly after the 'Torch Landings'.

Below: Headed by a standard bearer, US troops advance on an airfield near Algiers on the day of the 'Torch Landings'.

Italy Surrenders

Following the Allied success in Africa, it was agreed at the Trident
Conference in Washington to launch an attack on Italy, hoping to remove
the country from the war and provide access to Europe and the Balkans.
Sicily was to be the first target. The invasion, codenamed 'Operation
Husky', began on 10th July 1943 and, although there were around 400,000
Axis troops stationed there, the island was conquered within six weeks.
Messina was the last city to fall on 17th August. By this time, the Fascist
government in Italy had fallen. Mussolini was ousted and arrested, and had
been replaced by Marshal Pietro Badoglio who began negotiations for
Italian withdrawal from the war. On 3rd September the Allies crossed over
to the Italian mainland and, on the 8th, an armistice was signed following
Italy's unconditional surrender. However, much of the country remained
under German control and, on 15th September, Mussolini was liberated
from house arrest by German troops. Allied forces continued to fight for
Italy's major cities, taking Naples at the beginning of October and
launching an assault on Rome. On the 13th, Italy declared war on
Germany, but resistance was sustained for the remainder of the year, with
Germany maintaining defensive positions throughout the country. Perhaps
the most important of these was the 'Gustav Line', which ran from coast
to coast, south of Rome.

Above: Italian soldiers
in Sicily surrender.

Opposite: First news
of Italy's surrender
reaches London.

Allied Air Offensive

Britain had been running bombing
raids against German cities from as
early as 1940 in retribution for the
Blitz attacks, and as a means of
weakening the German war
machine. In January 1943 Churchill
and Roosevelt decided to combine
British and American bombing raids
on Germany, and Axis occupied
territories, in a wider, more
sustained effort to disrupt,
demoralise and weaken the enemy.

Right: A US bomber
attacking grounded
Japanese planes in New
Guinea.

Below: US Liberator
bombers at an American
air base in England.

The Dambusters

On 17th May 1943, the RAF attacked, and successfully breached, two Ruhr dams with 'bouncing bombs'. These spherical devices are probably the most celebrated invention of Barnes Wallis, an aircraft engineer and designer who went on to develop various specialised bombs.

Below: The Mohne Dam, successfully breached following an attack in a Dambuster raid.

Left: The computerised gunsight of a Flying Fortress which was able to account for factors such as range and windspeed, ensuring greater accuracy even in difficult conditions.

Above: Air raids on Britain, though less
frequent and usually on a relatively
small scale, had not entirely ceased by
1943. These boys take tea in the
garden of their damaged home
following a raid in March.

Siege of Leningrad Continues

Above: A Russian soldier takes cover amongst rubble in Leningrad where the siege continued. At the beginning of 1943 up to 5,000 people were dying each day in the city, mainly due to starvation and disease. By the spring thaw supplies were getting through by sea, boosted by the American extension of Lend-Lease to Russia. Refugees were also being evacuated, but the death rate remained high.

The Eastern Front

In early January 1943 Russia demanded that the Axis forces, under control of the newly-promoted Field Marshal Paulus, surrender Stalingrad. However, acting on direct orders from Hitler he refused, despite the fact that his forces were now under siege themselves and running low on food and ammunition. In response, the Red Army launched a massive assault on German units to the south-west of the city on the 30th, effectively wiping them out, and the following day, Paulus and his army of some 90,000 men surrendered. The Axis forces had lost around 150,000 troops during the campaign, whilst Russian casualties stood at close to half-a-million. It was now clear that Germany was not invincible and, following the decisive victory at Stalingrad, the Russian offensive quickly gathered momentum.

Above: A Red Army patrol launches a counter-attack on the outskirts of Leningrad.

Opposite top: Russian troops capture a German tank as it attempts to penetrate defences in the city of Stalingrad.

Opposite below: Refugees in the battered streets of Stalingrad.

By mid-February, Russia had retaken Kursk, Rostov and Kharkov and continued to successfully oppose German counter-attacks. In July, with new Panther and Tiger tanks, Germany attempted to launch a blitzkrieg strike in the area around Kursk, but Russian intelligence enabled the Red Army to pre-empt the assault, leading to the largest tank battle of the war. After just five days of extremely intense fighting, the Germans had lost two-thirds of their tanks, and on 12th July they were to lose 350 tanks and more than 10,000 men, once again forcing them to go on the defensive. Before the year was out, Russia had severely weakened German forces and would regain Smolensk and Kiev. As winter approached, Russia's war industries were now working at full speed, and the Red Army was preparing for major campaigns across the country. Leningrad, however, remained besieged.

The Warsaw Uprising of 1943

Warsaw in Poland had been turned into a Jewish ghetto by the occupying Germans, from which hundreds of thousands of Jews were taken to death camps during the war. However, in January 1943, partisan fighters of the ZOB, or Jewish Fighting Organisation began to resist attempts to deport people from the city. Inspired by some successes in April, over 700 fighters with a small supply of smuggled weapons, began a revolt against German troops which lasted almost a month. The uprising was eventually quashed and thousands of the city's inhabitants were executed, whilst many more were removed to concentration camps.

Above: Men, women and children taken from a building at gunpoint, following the failed uprising.

Convoys

The Battle of the Atlantic came to a climax by May 1943. In the winter months up until February, losses to the North Atlantic convoys had been somewhat reduced, but the German U-boat fleet continued to grow and, coupled with a breakdown in Allied intelligence in March, German submarines began once more to inflict heavy loses on the convoys, particularly in the mid-Atlantic gap where shipping could not be protected by air cover. That month, approximately 475,000 tons of shipping was lost, and Britain's lifeline was almost severed. However, by April, a dramatic increase in air support, and in the number of escort vessels, meant that Allied sinkings fell to around half the number of the previous month. At the same time, with improved radar systems, effective intelligence, and more VLR (Very Long Range) aircraft, U-boat losses began to rise. By the end of May almost 100 submarines had been destroyed, and the remainder of the U-boat fleet was withdrawn. From the summer onwards the rate of shipbuilding surpassed the rate at which the Germans were able to effect losses and, although the U-boats would return to the North Atlantic in the autumn with improved weaponry and radar, some 40 of them were destroyed in the last four months of the year.

Above: A German submarine pictured just moments before being sunk by US Liberator bombers.

US Air Force

The US air force initially favoured performing daylight raids over Europe to ensure greater precision, even on long-range missions when distances precluded fighter support. During 1942 and the early months of 1943 part of their success could be attributed to the fact that much of the German fighter force was in Russia and North Africa. However, during the summer of 1943 American losses soared. German defences had been much improved, and their fighter pilots learned to attack bombers head-on, taking advantage of poor frontal defences. In turn, the Americans were prompted to devise the means of surmounting these problems. Amongst the most important developments was detachable 'drop tanks', (*below*) which allowed extra fuel to be carried by supporting fighter planes on long-range bombing missions. By early 1944 US fighters were accompanying bombers as far as Berlin, and in the event of an engagement with enemy fighter planes, the fuel tanks could simply be discarded.

Above: Improved targeting systems enabled these US bombers to strike even through dense cloud.

Opposite: A B17 Flying Fortress crew study the new remote-controlled chin-turret which provided better protection against frontal fighter assaults.

Italy 1944

The Allies made little progress in the first few months after landing in Italy, gaining only around 70 miles in the face of heavy resistance, particularly at Monte Cassino and along the, Gustav Line, south of Rome. In early 1944 attacks were launched at these locations, whilst a new assault began with landings at Anzio. These campaigns produced little success until May when the Allies finally breached the 'Gustav Line'. The Eighth and Fifth Armies, joined by the US Sixth Corps, were able to drive the Germans back – first to a position north of Rome and later to the 'Gothic Line' north of Florence in June. Throughout the autumn attacks were launched against the 'Gothic Line' towards Rimini and Bologna, and ground was slowly gained over the remainder of the year.

Above and right: A German soldier in northern Italy waves a white flag of surrender from within his 'fox hole' and emerges into the custody of Polish troops.

'The Heavies'

The US B17 Flying Fortress was amongst the most effective bombers of the conflict, flying more combat missions than any other bomber, and serving in every theatre of war throughout the conflict. It was also produced in the largest numbers, with some 12,726 being manufactured between 1935 and 1939. The B17 was held in high regard due to its toughness and ability to withstand enemy fire, but several were downed, mainly during daylight raids. *Above:* Crew members of the 'Little Twink' are reunited after their plane was shot down over Germany. Only two of the seven that bailed out survived, whilst the pilot and two others rode out a crash landing.

Left: Despite massive damage to the tail of this B17, the pilot managed to return from his bombing mission over Germany to execute a perfect landing back in Britain.

Above: Part of a massive
formation of US bombers
return from a raid in
Germany.

Right: The ground crew of
the 'Hell's Angels' attend
to their plane, a veteran
bomber of the Eighth Air
Force, and one of the
most prolific Flying
Fortresses of the war.

Above: American tank crews on manoeuvres in England, February 1944.

Left: US airmen report back to an officer following a successful raid on industrial sites near Berlin. The markings on the back of this navigator's jacket indicate the number of missions he has completed.

Russia 1944

In 1944 the Russian offensive continued to gain momentum throughout the country, the objective being to completely wipe out, or drive back, all enemy forces from the region. By the end of January, Leningrad was finally liberated from a siege that had lasted some 900 days, and the German Army Group North retreated to the Baltic States as the Red Army pushed on towards Estonia and Latvia. Further south meanwhile, successful assaults saw the Russians regaining ever more ground, crossing into former Poland and Romania. By April, the task of clearing the Crimea was underway, with Odessa recaptured on the 10th, and the entire Ukraine regained in May. During the summer, campaigns continued into Finland and through Lithuania, whilst Minsk fell in early July, with the capture of 100,000 German troops.

By August almost all of Russia had been liberated. Encouraged by the Russians, who were on the outskirts of Warsaw, the partisan Polish Home Army began an uprising on 1st August, but the Red Army failed to intervene, and actively prevented Allied help getting through by refusing to permit the use of its airfields. In the ensuing massacre some 200,000 Poles are estimated to have died. The Russian drive was far from over, however, and for the remainder of the year the Red Army continued to fight through the Baltic region and the Balkans, gradually securing peace with Finland, Romania, Bulgaria and Hungary, who in turn declared war upon Germany.

Above: Russian soldiers watch their troops advance against the German line from the hills above a battlefield.

Pacific War

At Churchill and Roosevelt's meeting at Casablanca in January 1943, it was agreed that two main offensives be simultaneously launched in the Pacific: one through the Solomon Islands, and the other along the coast of Papua New Guinea, with the intention of opening a route through to the Philippines. In mid-January, around five months after US troops landed on Gaudalcanal, the Japanese began withdrawing some 10,000 troops, but the fighting there remained intense until the Japanese evacuation was completed in early February.

Meanwhile, by the end of January, the Allies gained the advantage in Papua New Guinea and made plans to take control of surrounding islands. Naval battles continued to be fought in the area, but it was evident that the Japanese had lost control of the south-west Pacific. A further blow to the Japanese was struck when the commander of the combined fleet, Admiral Yamamoto, was shot down in an aircraft above the Solomons. Throughout the summer US and Australian forces made progress through the Solomon and Aleutian Islands, but Japanese resistance was consistently fierce. However, by the end of August, both the central Solomons and the Aleutian Islands were in Allied control and a new 'island-hopping' campaign was opened up in the Central Pacific, through the Gilbert Islands towards the Marshall Island group. Fighting continued in New Guinea throughout the year, but the mainly Australian troops continued to drive northwards, pushing the Japanese back.

Above: General Frank Merrill and some of his staff discuss new methods to hamper the Japanese at headquarters somewhere in the Burmese jungles.

Burma

The Japanese invasion of Burma in 1942 had successfully
cut off supply routes to China along the Burma Road,
and placed Japanese troops dangerously close to the Indian
border. Japanese commanders had hoped that Indian forces
in the area would revolt against the British. However,
although some captured soldiers were formed into an
army to fight against the Allies, colonial Indian divisions,
which had fought alongside British troops in North
Africa, were redeployed to Burma in 1943 where they
fought with great distinction. Now under the overall
command of Lord Mountbatten, British troops were
reinforced and received greater air support, enabling them
to maintain defensive positions deep in the Burmese
jungles, and the employment of guerrilla tactics would
result in some successful campaigns against the Japanese.
Major General Orde Wingate formed and led the 77th
Indian Infantry Brigade, otherwise known as the 'Chindits',
who adopted the tactic of 'Long Range Penetration',
operating in columns deep inside enemy territory,
sabotaging infrastructure and ambushing Japanese troops.
Although they were eventually ordered to withdraw as air-
drops became more difficult, the 'Chindits' had proved
that damage could be inflicted on the Japanese in difficult
jungle territory.

Above: A scout group comprising
British, American, Chinese and
native Kachin troops operating in
the Burmese jungle.

Raids on Germany

The bombing raids unleashed upon Germany became increasingly intensive as the war progressed, and the Allies began to adopt a more offensive strategy. Their targets were generally industry or infrastructure and included transport networks, docks and factories. However, during the night-time raids on cities, accuracy could not always be guaranteed and many civilian lives were lost. In the major campaign against Hamburg in July 1943, over 40,000 civilians are thought to have perished as the city was relentlessly bombed day and night for a week. More accurate raids were also conducted, such as that on the rocket research facility at Peenemunde in August, which although it did not destroy the base, certainly delayed development and production of the flying bombs that would later be used against Britain.

Above and opposite below: Bombs plunge towards targets in Berlin.

Right: A huge bombed-out area shows the scale of the damage in this part of Berlin.

In the autumn of 1943, mass raids were launched against
Berlin. Air Marshal 'Bomber' Harris had long believed that
the destruction of several major German cities would be
enough to end the war. Although the RAF and USAF had
inflicted serious damage on Germany, and no doubt forced
the military to direct resources away from offensive
campaigns, the losses of Allied planes and crewmen were
also severe. Over a four-month period in 1943, more than
1,000 bombers and their crews were lost.

However, in 1944, with the advent of the US long-range
P-51D Mustang fighter, the Allied raiders, particularly the
Americans who continued to fly daylight missions, were
guaranteed a little more protection.

Above: Factories and an
airfield in Berlin burn after
heavy bombing.

Right: A Nazi flag draped
over Berlin ruins to
commemorate Hitler's 55th
birthday in April 1944.

Above: Bombs exploding across a wide area of Berlin, striking the Templehof marshalling yards, Anhalter Station and other parts of the railway system.

Left: This US A-20 Havoc bursts into flames having sustained hits from anti-aircraft guns over France in May 1944.

CHAPTER FOUR

D-Day to Peace

Throughout the winter of 1943 and the spring of 1944, preparations for the invasion of France were proceeding apace in Britain. The abortive raid on Dieppe in 1942 had proved that it was virtually impossible to capture and hold a major French port, and therefore 'Operation Overlord' was planned to land on the less well-defended Normandy beaches east of the Cherbourg peninsula. Technology was employed to overcome the problems of landing and supplying a vast invasion force without the benefit of a captured port. Special landing craft were built, amphibious vehicles were invented and artificial 'Mulberry' harbours would be towed across the channel. The oil this enormous army would need was to be pumped directly through 'PLUTO', a pipeline laid across the seabed from the Isle of Wight to Normandy.

The overall commander, General Eisenhower, gave the order for the long-awaited attack to commence on 6th June 1944: D-Day. Decoy activity in the Calais area fooled the Germans into believing an attack was imminent along that part of the coast, and soon after midnight parachutists and glider-borne troops landed behind German lines in Normandy. Simultaneously, a vast invasion fleet of over 4,000 vessels closed in on the beaches. At first light, with cover from thousands of aircraft, the invasion began and by the end of the first day 130,000 men had been put ashore.

ATTEMPT TO ASSASSINATE HITLER

Plans for increasing and supplying the invasion force were successful and, on 27th June, American forces captured the port of Cherbourg. On 8th July Caen fell and the Allies pushed out of Normandy towards Paris. German forces were not prepared for such an attack and it now seemed that their defeat was within sight, a defeat that would no doubt have been hastened had the Stauffenberg Plot been successful. On 20th July a group of German generals attempted to assassinate Hitler by placing a bomb under a table at his headquarters in East Prussia. He escaped virtually unscathed, however, and all those involved in the conspiracy were executed.

FRANCE LIBERATED

On 15th August a second invasion force landed in the south of France near Toulon and drove the Germans north along the Rhone valley. In all their advances the Allies were given invaluable assistance by the French Resistance, who harried the retreating Germans.

Paris was liberated on 24th August and General de Gaulle led a symbolic march along the Champs-Elysées through deliriously happy crowds.

A BRIDGE TOO FAR?

By September the Allies had reached Belgium, and Antwerp and Brussels had been recaptured. American troops passed through Belgium and reached the German border. The great obstacle to further advances into Germany itself was the Rhine, and it was in the hope of seizing vital bridgeheads that General Montgomery devised 'Operation Market Garden'. This was an audacious attempt to land airborne troops behind German lines and capture important crossing points. The early stages of the operation were a success, but the British 1st Airborne Division met with strong German resistance at Arnhem in the Netherlands, and troops sent to relieve them were held up. After a heroic action they were withdrawn with heavy casualties and the Rhine remained under German control.

In December the Germans launched a counter-attack in the Ardennes, which pushed the Allies back some 40 miles. On account of the bulge it created into Allied lines, this became known as the 'Battle of the Bulge'.

RED ARMY ADVANCES

Whilst Allied forces were liberating Western Europe, the Russians had been advancing relentlessly from the east. On 3rd July they took Minsk, capturing 100,000 German soldiers, and by the end of the month they had advanced into Western Poland. On 1st August 1944 the Warsaw uprising began, when the Polish resistance rose against the German garrison. Stalin halted the Russian advance, leaving the anti-communist insurgents to their fate. The Germans took a terrible revenge and 200,000 Poles died.

DOODLEBUGS ATTACK LONDON

By mid-1944 it was obvious that the defeat of Germany was inevitable, but Hitler refused to countenance surrender. Instead, he placed his faith in a new generation of secret weapons that would inflict devastating damage on Britain. From June onwards, the first of these, the V1, a pilotless flying bomb, began falling on London and South East England. They caused heavy damage, casualties and a dip in the morale of a population that felt that the Blitz had passed. The danger from the V1, or 'Doodlebug', decreased as Allied advances overran their launch sites in Northern France. It is estimated that between June and early September, almost 7,000 of these missiles were launched and over half were destroyed before reaching their intended targets. From September onwards, London came under attack from another new weapon, the V2. These were long-range rockets, fired from sites in territories still occupied by Germany. One effect of this renewed aerial onslaught was to revive the need to evacuate children from those areas threatened by attack, and by the end of July some 200,000 mothers and their children had left the capital.

Right: Part of the huge Allied fleet which crossed the channel on D-Day, 6th June 1944.

ALLIES 'ISLAND HOP' TO JAPAN

As events unfolded in Europe, the war continued unabated in the Far East. In March 1944 the Japanese launched an attack from Burma aimed at taking the Indian fortress of Imphal, but they were held up by British, Indian and Gurkha forces. These Allied forces went on the offensive in June and the Japanese were forced back into Burma, suffering appalling casualties whilst enduring the worst defeat suffered by a Japanese army in the field. The Allies received assistance from the American General Stillwell and were successful in re-opening the Burma Road, which allowed supplies in from China.

The Americans continued to fight back in the Pacific, pursuing the policy of 'island-hopping' towards Japan and, on 19th–20th June, the Battle of the Philippine Sea took place between fleets of aircraft carriers, during which neither fleet sighted the other. The Americans, with few losses, inflicted grievous damage to Japanese air and naval power in the Pacific and opened the way to the recapture of the Philippines.

ALLIES ADVANCE THROUGH GERMANY

As German might began to crumble, events unfolded relatively quickly in the opening months of 1945. Throughout January Russian armies advanced remorselessly upon Germany from the east, liberating the Nazi concentration camp at Auschwitz on the 27th. It was by now obvious that the final defeat of

Germany was imminent and, between 4th–11th February, Roosevelt, Churchill and Stalin met at Yalta in the Crimea to discuss the post-war division of Germany. On 14th April the Red Army took Vienna before turning its attention to Berlin. The Russians crossed the Oder and two armies encircled Berlin on 25th April. They joined to the west and then turned back towards the beleaguered city.

Further west, the Allies pushed on to the Rhineland and, on 7th March, American troops captured the bridge at Remegen intact, establishing a bridgehead across the river. Other Allied crossings were achieved and their forces penetrated deep into Germany. By 12th April an American column was just sixty miles from Berlin.

Throughout this period, British and American planes continued to bomb increasingly defenceless German targets. The most controversial of these attacks took place on the 13th–14th February, when the Allies launched a devastating raid on the beautiful medieval city of Dresden. The city had not previously been a target and was packed with refugees fleeing from the Russian advance in the east. The city was flattened and 135,000 people were killed.

CONCENTRATION CAMP HORRORS EXPOSED

As the Allies pressed eastwards, the full horror of the Nazi treatment of the Jewish population of Europe became apparent with the liberation of the concentration camps at Bergen-Belsen, Buchenwald and Dachau in April. Vast piles of corpses and starving survivors gave an indication of the scale of the Holocaust, in which some 6 million Jews and hundreds of thousands of other people lost their lives.

VICTORY IN EUROPE

In Italy, the war was also drawing to an end. The ex-dictator Benito Mussolini and his mistress Clara Petacci were captured and executed by partisans near Mezzegra and their bodies, along with fifteen others, were hung upside-down from the girders of a petrol station in Milan. The war in the Mediterranean ended on 2nd May 1945 when the German commander in Italy surrendered.

Meanwhile, American forces had advanced to the Elbe and met up with the Russians. At the same time, Russian troops were fighting their way through the

streets of Berlin block-by-block towards the Reichstag. On 30th April, after nominating Admiral Karl Doenitz as his successor, Hitler and his new wife Eva Braun committed suicide. The following day, having supervised the deaths of their six children, Josef Goebbels and his wife followed their example.

In the days that followed, German armies began to surrender and, on 7th May, General Eisenhower formally accepted the unconditional surrender of Germany. On the 8th Britain celebrated VE Day.

WAR CONTINUES IN THE FAR EAST

Although the fighting in Europe was now over, the war against Japan continued. British forces sustained their drive against Japanese troops in Burma, liberating the country from Japanese control on 2nd August 1945.

The American push through the Pacific was bringing them ever closer to Japan. In February they had taken Manila and the strategically important islands of Iwo Jima, only about 700 miles from Tokyo. However, the nearer the Americans came to the Japanese mainland, the more fanatical became the resistance of Japanese forces. The climax was reached in the battle for the island of Okinawa. When the Japanese abandoned it on 1st June, 110,000 out of 120,000 of their troops had been killed or had committed suicide, and 4,000 planes had been lost, the majority of which had been flown by Kamikaze pilots.

BUILDING A NEW BRITAIN

From the beginning of 1945, the people of Britain knew that the war was all but won, but the country still endured considerable hardship. Food remained in short supply and there was no end in sight to the rationing of food, clothing, furniture or fuel. As a result of bombing, the nation's housing stock was also severely depleted. Despite these problems, there was a great desire amongst the population for a return to normality and evacuees began to go back to the cities, whilst the first of the troops to be 'demobbed' returned home too.

People also eagerly awaited the first general election for 10 years. Polling day was 5th July, but as millions of voters remained overseas, it was three weeks before the result was known. To many people's amazement, there was a landslide victory for the Labour Party and Clement Atlee replaced Churchill as Prime Minister. He led a government that promised to introduce a welfare state and to nationalise major industries.

THE ULTIMATE WEAPON

On the 17th July 1945 the Allied leaders met at Potsdam near Berlin. President Roosevelt had died on 12th April and so it was that Churchill and Stalin met with the new President, Harry Truman. During the conference the new British Prime Minister, Clement Atlee, replaced Churchill. The leaders agreed to pursue the unconditional surrender of Japan.

By this time, Truman knew that America possessed a new deadly weapon: the atomic bomb. The Japanese refused to countenance unconditional surrender and Truman was advised that an assault on the Japanese mainland could result in up to one million American casualties. He therefore took the momentous decision to use the bomb.

On 6th August 1945 an American B29 Superfortress, the Enola Gay, flew high above the Japanese city of Hiroshima and dropped an atomic bomb that exploded above the city with devastating effects. Hiroshima was destroyed and over 78,000 people were instantly killed. Three days later a second bomb was dropped over the city of Nagasaki, killing 24,000.

The previous day, on 8th August, Russia had declared war on Japan and invaded Manchuria. This meant that, following the two atomic bombs, Japanese cities were now also subjected to heavy conventional bombing raids. On the 14th August the Japanese surrendered without conditions, the formal agreement being signed on 2nd September.

NUREMBURG TRIALS

When the war was over, there was widespread agreement that Nazi leaders should be brought to trial as war criminals. Some had escaped in the confusion of the final days of the conflict, and Hitler, Goebbels and Himmler had avoided justice by committing suicide. Those who had been captured were brought before an International War Crimes Court, which met at Nuremburg in November 1945 and was to last for several months. Of the twenty-one defendants, three were acquitted, seven received prison sentences ranging from ten years to life and the remainder were sentenced to death.

Of those to be executed, the most notable were Goering and the German Foreign Minister, Joachim von Ribbentrop. Hours before he was due to be hanged, Goering committed suicide by swallowing a cyanide capsule which he had kept hidden throughout the trial. On 16th October 1946 the executions of the others took place. Their bodies, together with that of Goering, were taken to Munich to be cremated and, according to the official announcement, their ashes were 'scattered in a river somewhere in Germany'.

Left: Young German soldiers captured just days after the Allied invasion of France.

Operation Overlord

From 6.30 am on 6th June, following the overnight deployment of
three airborne divisions constituting over 20,000 men, five assault
divisions began to land on their designated Normandy beaches,
codenamed Utah, Omaha, Gold, Juno and Sword. Throughout the
day over 130,000 Allied troops were landed on the beaches, from
around 7,000 vessels, with air-cover provided by some 12,000
aircraft. German troops, caught by surprise and poorly organised,
managed only one significant counter-attack, and by midnight the
landing points had been secured, in most cases with fewer casualties
than had been expected. At Omaha Beach, however, fierce German
resistance and a lack of cover caused terrible losses.

Above: The Allied fleet
approaches the Normandy
coast.

Opposite: Troops wade onto
the beach during the
Normandy landings.

Opposite above: British troops regroup on the beach at Ouistreham, codenamed Sword, before advancing inland.

Opposite below: British troops securing a beach following the initial landings. General Rommel had overseen the construction of 'The Atlantic Wall', with the deployment of over 6 million mines along the beaches from the Netherlands to the Spanish border, as well as obstructions designed to damage tanks and boats, and hamper infantry. At certain points, the coastline was even more heavily defended, with massive concrete revetments and trench systems, protected by large calibre weaponary.

Above: American troops approach the beach in a landing craft. At Omaha in particular, many men were killed before even managing to disperse from these vessels.

Above: American soldiers
training in preparation for
the D-Day landings. The
amount of planning which
had proceeded the operation
was probably the single most
important factor in its
success.

Right: Troops and supplies
moving inland from a secured
beachhead.

Above: Under the supervision of GIs, captured German prisoners carry an injured comrade as they prepare to be taken back to detention camps in Britain.

Allies Advance Into Northern France

After landing, the Allied forces quickly secured the beaches, enabling
rapid resupply and reinforcement. German forces were unprepared for
such a large scale invasion and, despite resistance, the Allied advance
into Northern France was relatively swift. The British pushed on to
Caen where fierce fighting would rage until 20th July. The conflict
and initial heavy shelling left the city ruined, but liberated.
Meanwhile, the Americans, who had landed further west on beaches
codenamed Omaha and Utah, captured the Cherbourg Peninsula.

Above: A German
soldier surrenders
having been captured
by American GIs.

Left: The Curé of Caen amidst the ruins.

Below: A column of German POWs marched through Cherbourg by American troops.

Second Invasion Front

As the Allies broke out of Northern France, the Germans were put under further pressure in August by a second invasion in the south, codenamed 'Dragoon'. This consisted of mainly American and Free French troops. They pushed on through the Rhone Valley to rendezvous with units from Normandy who were now driving the German forces eastwards.

Although the Allied invasion and subsequent campaign to reclaim France had required a great deal of air support, the attacks on Berlin persisted. In this raid (*right*), government buildings, including Hitler's Chancellery, are thought to have been hit.

Below: Red Cross aid for the advancing Allied forces

Above: Battles continued to devastate parts of Normandy as German resistance persisted. The town of St-Lô was particularly badly affected.

Left: A house-to-house search in progress amongst the ruins of May-sur-Orne.

Above: As the Allies advanced
through France, liberating towns as
they went, they had to clear a way
through the rubble of destroyed
buildings and other obstructions,
much of which had been deliberately
used by German forces to hinder
progress by Allied troops.

Right: The church at Aunay-sur-
Odon is badly damaged, but the
spire remains intact despite the
surrounding devastation.

Opposite: General Leclerc's armoured
division passes through the Arc de
Triomphe.

Paris Liberated

Although the Allied plan had originally been to bypass Paris, as Allied troops crossed the Seine to the north of the city, Parisians began a revolt against the occupying Germans on 19th August, and Allied units moved in to support them. Free French troops entered Paris and the city was liberated on the 25th. General de Gaulle led an Allied march along the Champs Elysées as crowds lined the route.

Left: Marking the liberation of Paris, the first edition of the *Continental Daily Mail* to have been printed since June 1940 is published on 28th August.

MONDAY. AUGUST 28, 1944.

Daily Mail

CONTINENTAL EDITION

The Continental "DAILY MAIL" reappears this morning - the first British newspaper to resume publication in Paris. It is in abbreviated form, but it is an earnest of the happier days that have come to Paris and many liberated areas of France.

This edition ends the gap in publication which began on Monday, June 10, 1940, the last publication date of the Continental "Daily Mail" in Paris before the German occupation.

For this edition special stories have been written by two brilliant "DAILY MAIL" writers :

Alexander CLIFFORD, who reported the BRITISH 8TH ARMY'S magnificent victory in North Africa and is now with the BRITISH ARMY in France.

Noel MONKS. who was well known to Continental "Daily Mail" readers before the war.

Liberation Edition

German 7th Army's Huge Losses

BY ALEXANDER CLIFFORD

Normandy, Sunday.

The freeing of Paris was one of the most exhilarating moments of history. And it is natural that it should have overshadowed the fact that the German Seventh Army is still being defeated in

SALUTE THESE MEN

The liberators of Paris were the troops of General Hodges' First American Army which included the 2nd French Armoured Division. This news was officially released last night, and with it the story of a gesture of courtesy made by General Hodges.

A letter was prepared as the official document which will shortly hand back the control of Paris from the American

Stirring Scenes at Liberation of Paris

BY NOEL MONKS

Paris, Sunday.

I came into Paris with an American advance column at noon on Friday, and I confess unashamedly that as we rounded a corner south of the Porte d'Italie and I saw the Eiffel Tower standing clear and

Although the city had been effectively freed from German control, Hitler had ordered Paris be defended to the last man and pockets of resistance remained. Whilst Allied troops were greeted with celebrations in the heart of the city, fighting continued in some areas and hidden snipers made attacks on Allied troops, including an attempt to assassinate General de Gaulle at Notre Dame.

Left: German soldiers captured in Paris.

Below: A scene of celebration as Allied troops join civilians on the streets.

Opposite: A French tank stands before the Arc de Triomphe as the capital is reclaimed.

Above: American GIs march through the centre of Paris along the Champs Elysées.

Right: A captured German prisoner is insulted by a member of the crowd as he is marched through the streets of St-Mihiel at gunpoint.

Opposite: The tricolour flying from the spire of Rouen Cathedral rises above the wreckage of the ruined city.

Operation Market Garden

By September, Allied forces were advancing into
Belgium and Luxembourg and plans were being put
in place to secure the Rhineland and Ruhr in
readiness for an assault on Holland and then
Germany itself. General Eisenhower, who was in
overall control of the Allied forces in Europe,
favoured maintaining a wide offensive line along
the whole of the front, but as the advance slowed,
he looked to Generals Patton and Montgomery,
who were controlling forces in the region, for
suggestions. There was some argument over what
form an such assault should take. Patton wished to
attack along the heavily defended Siegfried Line to
capture Metz, whilst Montgomery wished to
bypass these defences, cross the Rhine at Arnhem
and capture the German 15th Army from behind
their lines, whilst also cutting off the launch sites
from which V1 and V2 rockets were being fired at
London and other cities. The final plan was
Operation Market Garden, which involved
dropping paratroopers into the region in advance
of infantry and armoured divisions in an attempt
to secure vital crossing points across the Rhine.
Bridges were successfully secured at Veghel, Grave
and Nijmegen, but the British 1st Airborne and
Polish 1st Independent Parachute Brigade suffered
heavy casualties at Arnhem after troops sent to
relieve them failed to break through German
defences.

Left: A German soldier is captured on the road to Brussels by a Welsh corporal.

Below: British tanks pour into Belgium watched by a row of German prisoners.

Opposite above: Free French troops move in to secure a building being defended by hundreds of German troops.

Opposite below: Allied paratroops deployed over the lower Rhineland.

Brussels Liberated

By 2nd September, the Allies had liberated Brussels, and were moving across Belgium towards Germany. With their freedom restored, Belgian civilians and reistance groups began to round up German troops and Nazi sympathisers.

Left: The Belgian resistance was known as the White Army and, with Allied assistance, they played an important role in securing the country. The Allies drop supplies such as arms and ammunition to support them.

Below: An Allied transport convoy crossing a pontoon bridge on a Belgian river.

Opposite above: A group of prisoners brought in by Belgian resistance fighters.

Opposite below: Belgian police and civilians round up a group of 'Quislings', or Nazi sympathisers. The name was derived from Vidkun Quisling, a Norwegian politician who had collaborated with the Nazis following the German invasion of Norway in 1940.

Bruges Liberated

The old town of Bruges was liberated by Canadian forces around 15th September, and despite days of fighting, the town itself was unscathed.

Left: A Belgian who had worked for the Gestapo is captured and handcuffed by police in Grammont.

Below: British tanks moving into the Belgian capital are cheered on by locals.

Opposite above: Canadian troops welcomed into Bruges.

Opposite below: A British armoured squadron supports troops holding a bridgehead near Gheel in Belgium where German resistance was fierce.

Right: British tanks and their crews are mobbed by ecstatic Belgians as they pass through Brussels.

Below: Similar scenes of jubilation as the Belgian Brigade, an independent infantry group formed in Britain, enter the city.

Above: As German troops retreated from Brussels they left the Palais de Justice burning in their wake.

Just days after Brussels was retaken, the Allies captured the port of Antwerp, taking German troops by surprise and cutting off their escape routes.

Left: A British soldier, accompanied by a local woman, marches a group of captured German troops through Antwerp.

Allies Into Germany

Although the operation at Arnhem was abandoned, the American successes in holding bridgeheads such as that over the Maas at Nijmegen in Holland enabled the Allies to cross into parts of Germany in late September, but crossing the Rhine was to remain the next major objective. Towards the end of the year, however, progress stalled once more, and Hitler was to seize the opportunity to regroup his forces and direct an attack through the Ardennes, with the intention of reclaiming Antwerp. The initial Panzer drive was a success, but by late December this 'bulge' in the Allied line had been contained and was beginning to be driven back.

Above: As heavy fighting continues during October, German refugees leave Aachen. American troops, meanwhile, head deeper into the town.

Left: Part of a British tank regiment near Nijmegen.

Opposite above: British troops in Brussels enjoy an ice cream.

Opposite below: US troops help to clear possessions from German homes set ablaze by Nazi incendiary bombs.

Italian Resistance

Whilst the Allied troops advanced
into the Low Countries and
Germany, conflict continued in
Italy. Despite the armistice signed
with the Italian government in
1943, German forces and Italians
loyal to Mussolini continued their
resistance.

Right: Italians loyal to
the Allies search for
enemy troops.

Above: British troops
advance towards the
town of Venray in
Holland.

Opposite above: British
troops moving swiftly
through the narrow
streets of Flushing in
Holland. Pockets of
resistance, particularly
enemy snipers, were a
constant threat as the
Allies regained control
of such towns and
closed in on Germany.

Opposite below: Germans
captured in Aachen.

Above and Opposite above: A long column of German troops files out of Aachen as they finally surrender the town to the Americans.

Opposite below: New Zealand Tempest pilots who had successfully defended England against German flying bombs, now based in Belgium.

Right: Germans
surrender a defensive
position to US troops
as the Allied advance
into Germany
continues.

Below: An oil refinery
near Gelsenkirchen in
Germany, devastated by
RAF and US Air
Force bombing.

The Allied drive into Germany was supported by constant bombing raids on industrial and military targets inside the country aimed at wiping out essential supply lines.

Left: Smoke billowing from multiple targets in Bergen.

Below: German mines being cleared.

Above: Cheering crowds are held back by police in Paris as Winston Churchill is awarded the freedom of the city.

Right: As the Allies moved across Europe they began to come across concentration camps where hundreds of thousands of prisoners had been murdered. This camp in Holland was now being used to house German prisoners.

Above: British and American tank crews enter Gelsenkirchen.

Above and right:
German troops held
out at Metz in
France until the end
of 1944, when the
last garrison was
surrendered to US
troops.

Refugees Head For Safety

Above: American troops move in to deal with the German counter-attack in Belgium in December 1944 as refugees head for the safety of the Allied lines.

Above: Mounted French
soldiers with German
prisoners.

Right: Bastoogne in Belgium
is liberated following a
German siege during the
'Battle of the Bulge' which
left the town in ruins.

Above: An anti-aircraft
gun employed to bring
down flying bombs
over Belgium.

Above: Part of a small infantry group of the US 82nd Airborne ambush a German patrol near Bra in Belgium.

Right: An anti-tank gun is towed into a recently captured Belgian town.

Battle of the 'Bulge'

Throughout the winter and spring, fighting continued in parts of Belgium in harsh weather as the Allies fought against a sixty-mile long 'bulge' of German reistance into the Allied front. By January, however, the German offensive was beginning to wane. The Allies took full advantage of the German collapse and resumed their advance almost immediately, pushing on towards the Rhine.

Above: German soldiers lie dead in the snow, cut down by machine gun fire as they attempted to overrun a command post at Bastogne.

Left: A German soldier killed by shelling, frozen rigid in the snow near Nefte.

Right: Mourners grieve at the funeral of 34 young Belgian men murdered on Christmas Eve in an atrocity by German soldiers. The men had been part of a forced labour group formed by the Germans when they re-took the town of Bande.

Below: Anhalter Station in Berlin, badly damaged by Allied bombing, as were almost all the buildings in the area.

Above: Members of
the Third US Army
commanded by
General Patton
advance on
Houffalize, Belgium,
during the 'Battle of
the Bulge'.

Left: These women,
manning an anti-
aircraft gun in
Belgium, are warmed
by thick winter coats
and a tot of rum.

Iwo Jima

Through 1944 into 1945, the Allies were also
successful in the Far East and Pacific regions,
as the Japanese suffered increasingly severe
losses both on land and at sea. British and
American forces reopened the Burma Road
after decimating Japanese forces in June. In the
same month the Battle of the Philippine Sea
established Allied naval superiority. The
American forces continued 'island hopping'
through the Pacific towards Japan, reclaiming
the Philippines and enduring some of the
worst fighting of the war on Iwo Jima and
the Ryukyu Islands, including Okinawa, where
fighting was to last for months.

Above: The US flag is
raised on Mount
Suribachi on Iwo Jima,
23rd February 1945.

Above: British and Dutch soldiers defending a bridge in Belgium as tanks head towards Germany.

Left: Although there were heavy snows, RAF bomber crews continued to operate from Belgium to support the Allied drive and weaken German resistance.

The 'Big Three' Meet

Right: Churchill and Stalin shake hands when the 'big three' meet at Yalta in the Crimea in February 1945. President Roosevelt is seated. With Allied success seemingly now assured, they were to discuss plans for the invasion of Japan and the partition of Germany.

Below and opposite above: Bombers relentlessly pounded Berlin as Allied troops closed in on the city. These US B-17s were part of a 1,000 bomber raid which unleashed 2,500 tons of bombs.

Left: With Brussels liberated it became an important base for the Allies in Europe. Here members of the various armed forces enjoy some rest and relaxation at the 21 Club.

Russians Advance in the East

Towards the end of March 1945 several vital crossings had
been established across the Rhine. Amongst the most
important of these was at Remagen, where the US First
Army was able to secure a railway bridge intact. In the East
the Russian advance on Germany was also gaining momentum,
and Eisenhower ordered the Allies to press on towards Berlin
with the aim of meeting up with the Red Army.

Above: Civilians in the German
city of Rheydt, birthplace of
Joseph Goebbels, emerge with
white flags as the Allies
approach, apparently unsure of
how they will be treated.

Above: As the US Third Army entered Bitburg they found fewer than 100 inhabitants remaining.

Left: Germans surrender in the city of Trier.

Italy 1945

In Italy 1945 the Eighth Army
continued to push forward in
preparation for the spring offensive. It
was launched in April, and proved to
be the decisive action in clearing the
Germans from the country. By the
end of the month Spezia, Genoa and
Venice had been liberated. Senior
German officers, who had been
engaged in secret negotiations with the
Allies to end the war in Italy since
February, signed a document of
unconditional surrender without
reference to Berlin. This was to take
effect from 2nd May. The cease-fire
took place as agreed, just as the Allies
were reaching Trieste.

Right: An American
Liberator bomber
plunges towards the
ground over Italy. Its
wing is severely damaged
by anti-aircraft fire.

Opposite above: Churchill crossing the Rhine with General Montgomery on an American craft.

Above: Winston Churchill with General Montgomery (left) and a US commander during a visit to the German town of Julich in March 1945, from where Generals Montgomery and Eisenhower were directing their operations.

Crossing the Rhine

Left: The retreating German forces operated a scorched earth policy, destroying roads and bridges as they went. As a result, Allied engineers established several crossing points on the Rhine, such as this floating pontoon bridge.

Below: The Allies were beginning to establish control in parts of Germany and civilians were encouraged to turn over weapons to local authorities. A German policeman, working under US supervision, records details of weapons which have been handed in.

Opposite: Churchill crossing a Bailey bridge over the Roer.

Resistance Folds

German resistance continued to fold as the Allied advance gained momentum in March and April 1945. Some cities such as Saarbrucken (*opposite above*), which had already been ravaged by bombing, fell without conflict on the ground. Of its pre-war population of around 135,000 inhabitants, less than 1,000 remained in 1945. Many gathered in the city's square as the Allies took possession.

Above: Young wounded German soldiers captured by the British following a battle at Millingen, where Montgomery's troops fought to maintain a bridgehead.

Opposite below: German prisoners taken by the US Third Army are interned in a former Nazi concentration camp.

Above: One of the youngest
German prisoners taken by the
Allies. This boy, not yet 15, was
captured in March as Allied troops
attacked the 'Siegfried Line'.

Allies Into Germany

With numerous crossing points secured, the Allies poured men across the Rhine in vast numbers in March 1945. Meanwhile, the Red Army continued its approach on Germany from the East, reclaiming several major Russian cities.

Above: British troops traverse the floodbank of the Rhine as they prepare to cross the river.

Left: Two artillery batteries lined up close to the banks of the Rhine in advance of a crossing, 24th March.

The Airborne Fleet

While infantry and armoured divisions crossed bridges on the Rhine at the end of March, thousands of airborne troops were deployed by the RAF to engage with German forces east of the river. The largest airborne fleet ever assembled for a single mission, stretching some 500 miles, carried thousands of paratroopers and towed hundreds of gliders into battle.

Right: Gliders being towed across the Rhine.

Below and opposite: Views of the vast air armada above Germany.

Above: The First
Airborne Division
parachute onto the
banks of the Rhine.

Right: An amphibious
vehicle makes a
crossing of the Rhine.

Victory In Sight

By the spring of 1945, with victory in sight, the Allied forces pressed home their advantage, mobilising troops into Germany along a huge front, with assaults towards Hamburg in the north, the Elbe in the centre, and in the south through Bavaria, Czechoslovakia and Austria, where they would ultimately be joined by Italian forces. By 14th April the Red Army had reached as far as Vienna in the south, and General Zuhkov's armies, advancing further north, had reached the Oder. It was his men who would lead the attack on Berlin, unleashing perhaps the largest artillery barrage in history on 15th April, when over a million shells were fired against German positions. Ten days later, Russian troops made contact with General Bradley's forces at Torgau, and by now the Russians had encircled Berlin, and began to move into the city.

Above: British troops move out from the eastern banks of the Rhine, heading past German dead.

Above: A column of
German prisoners stretches
into the distance. Fierce
battles raged through towns
east of the Rhine resulting
in the capture of thousands
of German soldiers.

Right: Machine guns
manned by commandos in
Wesel. British commandos
led one of the first
crossings across the Rhine
in assault craft, capturing
the town of Wesel and
taking over 300 prisoners
on 23rd March.

Street Fighting

Men of the Gordon Highlanders following
the fall of Rees (above). Montgomery's troops
crossed the Rhine to capture Rees where
vicious house-to-house fighting was to take
place in the town's narrow streets. From here
they would go on to capture the important
industrial area of the Ruhr.

Above: As the 15th Scottish Division move up towards the front line they pass a line of captured Germans headed for captivity in what is now Allied territory.

Left: A seemingly endless stream of supplies was brought across the Rhine to support the Allies as they pushed eastwards. Here a transport convoy crosses a Bailey pontoon bridge.

Opposite: The devastation in Rees.

Hitler's Final Rally

On the 30th March in a final and desperate attempt to rally both civilians and troops, Hitler issued the statement: 'Fanatic determination can guarantee the success of the coming fight. Then the battle before Berlin must and will end with a decisive defensive victory'. However, many German soldiers were by now ready to surrender, and they did so in their thousands.

Above: German soldiers taken prisoner by General Patton's forces march west where they are to be imprisoned in internment camps.

Opposite below: Some 20,000 German prisoners of war held in a former German military academy await processing.

Liberating POWs

As the Allies were establishing POW camps in Germany, they were liberating their own troops from others. Some of the prisoners that were rescued had been held captive since the outbreak of war.

Above: An American soldier, machine gun trained on the compound below, keeps a watchful eye as he guards German detainees.

Right: Russian prisoners liberated from Stalag 326-6K POW camp hold aloft an American soldier in celebration.

Above: German paratroopers put up a bitter defence in Emmerich in early April, but British and Canadian troops under Montgomery's command eventually succeeded in capturing the town.

Death Camps Uncovered

Stalag 11B was the first POW camp to be liberated that contained British soldiers. The men in this picture show clear signs of malnutrition, but this was nothing compared to the horrors uncovered when the Allies liberated the Nazi death camps, where literally millions of Jewish and other 'non-Aryan' people had been exterminated. It would be some time until the extent of Nazi atrocities and Hitler's attempt at genocide was fully realised. At Belsen, troops discovered some 60,000 civilians living in appalling conditions; almost all were starving and suffering from disease and many had been tortured. There were also 15,000 or 20,000 unburied corpses, and inmates were dying at a rate of around 500 a day.

Right: Joseph Kramer, who became known as the 'Beast of Belsen', was the only senior officer remaining at the camp. He was put on trial and hanged in December 1945.

Berlin Falls

Russian troops were the first to reach Berlin and they immediately became involved in fierce street fighting as they attempted to advance through the city towards the Reichstag. On 30th April Hitler committed suicide in his bunker below the Chancellery, and two days later Berlin was in the hands of the Russians.

Left: A Russian soldier in Berlin.

Above: Young German soldiers under guard.

German Guerillas

Above: A captured werewolf. German guerilla
units, known as 'werewolves', began to appear
behind Allied lines in the closing weeks of the
war. However, their numbers were small and by
this time it was too late for them to mount an
effective resistance.

Left: The Allies begin to exert powers of civil control, establishing a Military Government in British occupied Germany.
The first trials held by the Allies in Germany related to civilians crossing into Holland without authority. This man, Josef Gielen, was sentenced to six months imprisonment for the offence.

Below: German civilians turn over weapons to GIs in Usla. Several also hand over Nazi flags.

VE Day

The German unconditional surrender was made official on 7th May at General Eisenhower's HQ in Rheims, France. It was signed to take effect from midnight on the 8th, the day that would be celebrated as Victory in Europe, or VE Day. On the 9th the surrender was ratified in Berlin and signed for the Allies by Eisenhower's Deputy, A.C.M. Tedder and the Russian General, Marshal Zhukov. Fighting was to perist in Czechoslovakia for a further four days, but the conflict in Europe was effectively over.

Above: Street parties were held all over Britain in celebration of VE Day.

Opposite: Berlin in ruins, having sustained heavy bombing in advance of the Allied entry into the city.

Winston Churchill made his official VE
Day announcement on Tuesday, 8th May
from the balcony of the Ministry of
Health, (*below*) as crowds packed the
streets below. Although war continued in
the Pacific, Europe had now been
liberated after years of hardship and
uncertainty.

Right and opposite:
Celebrations in London.
Streamers were made from
the tickertape used to feed
news to Fleet Street.

Above: Crowds begin to
gather in Piccadilly Circus
in anticipation of the
official VE Day
proclamation.

Opposite above: Search lights which
once scanned for enemy aircraft
now light up the skies in
celebration over the Russian capital,
Moscow, as thousands of citizens
flock to Red Square.

Opposite below: The vast crowds
gathered in Trafalgar Square fall
silent in order to listen to
Churchill's announcement.

Right: Winston Churchill in the
grounds of Buckingham Palace
with the King. Churchill would
later make several appearances on
the Royal Balcony.

Below: An American Corporal,
assigned to a military police
platoon in Germany, holds an
inspection of female prisoners at a
camp in Magdeburg May 1945.
Over 200 women who had been
part of the German forces were
held there.

Above: A British sergeant, with his wife and son, is greeted by locals upon his return to a Devon villiage from a German POW camp.

Street Parties

Whilst the parties continued and the last remaining German forces surrendered across Europe, the four major Allied powers, Britain, Russia, the USA and France, moved into their zones of occupation in Germany to begin the long and serious task of reconstruction.

Above: A children's VE Day party in Brockley, South London.

Opposite: With flags strung between the houses and a 'V' for victory chalked on the cobbles, the residents of this street in Leeds prepare for a VE Day street party.

The Task Ahead

The Allies set about the task of reconstruction in
Germany, dealing with housing problems, food
shortages, reopening schools and other
administrative tasks. Information was mainly
conveyed to the German people through the
military government departments set up by
SHAEF, the Supreme Headquarters Allied
Expeditionary Force. However, other lines of
communication included standardised weekly
newspapers produced by the PWD, or
Psychological Warfare Division.

Above: A citizen of
Leipzig reads the
Hessische Post, a
publication produced
under direction of the
12th Army Group.

Right: Civilians in Berlin begin to clear the streets of rubble under direction from Russian troops.

Below: A Russian victory parade held in Red Square, Moscow, on 24th June.

Above and opposite: Berliners, mainly
women, work in chain gangs to clear
rubble from bombsites.

German Civilians

In May 1945 food was scarce in Germany and the typical ration for German civilians left many close to starving. However, those that were willing to work, particularly those involved in heavier duties such as construction, fared much better and were paid well enough to supplement their rations, whilst aiding the reconstruction of their cities.

Potsdam Conference

Although the people of Europe felt a great
weight lifted from their shoulders, the war
against Japan continued, and there was serious
business to discuss. In the second half of
June, the heads of the three great powers met
at Potsdam, near Berlin, to talk about the
future in Europe and to plan the campaign
against Japan. By the end of the conference,
of the original three major Allied wartime
leaders, only Stalin remained. President
Truman represented the United States for the
first time, and Winston Churchill was only
present at the outset, as the Conservative
Party lost the June election in Britain and
Labour's Clement Attlee, took over. The
Potsdam Declaration was broadcast on 26th
June and demanded Japan's unconditional
surrender.

Above: A huge portrait
of Stalin outside the
shell of the Adlon
hotel in Berlin.

Right: A young female
Russian soldier directs
traffic at the
Brandenburg Gate.

Above: Churchill meets British
commanders when he arrives
at Berlin Airport for the
Potsdam Conference.

Churchill Meets Truman

Above: Prime Minister Winston Churchill greets the new American President, Harry S. Truman, when they meet for the first time. Roosevelt had died on 12th April 1945, less than a month before Germany's surrender and, as Vice-President, Truman was sworn in. The meeting took place at Potsdam in July as the leaders continued to hone the details of the European peace process.

Above: The American Embassy (on the right) and the Brandenburg Gate in Berlin, both bearing the scars of battle.

Atom Bombs Vaporise Japanese Cities

From October 1944 until August 1945, Japan was bombed relentlessly as plans were formulated for an Allied invasion. American assaults switched from daylight precision raids to night-time area bombing, devastating Japanese cities with thousands of incendiaries. Fears of fanatical resistance and massive Allied casualties prompted President Truman to sanction the use of an atomic bomb.

Above: Nagasaki, almost completely levelled by the explosion.

Opposite: The vast mushroom cloud which rose some 20,000 feet above Nagasaki, the second Japanese city to be devastated by the use of the atomic bomb.

'My God, What Have We Done?'

At around 8.15am on 6th August, 'Little Boy' was dropped from B-29 bomber the *Enola Gay* on the Japanese city of Hiroshima. As the bomb burst at a height of over 2,000 feet, instantly killing tens of thousands of civilians, the plane filled with light and the co-pilot, Robert Lewis, turned to his crew asking: 'My God, what have we done?'. Three days later, 'Fat Man' was dropped on Nagasaki. Including those killed outright, 103,000 people are estimated to have died within four months of the bombings, with many further deaths attributed to the effects of radiation. Today, the health of over 90,000 survivors is still being monitored.

Above: The casing of an atomic bomb of the same type as 'Fat Man', on display in the USA.

Left: A selection of newspapers from across the United States during the week of the bombings.

Opposite: Scenes of destruction at Hiroshima.

VJ Day

On 15th August, after almost six years of conflict, Emperor Hirohito was to broadcast the announcement of Japan's unconditional surrender, bringing the Second World War to an end. However, the celebrations that followed were more muted than those of VE Day, no doubt as the world reeled in shock at the devastation wrought by the atomic bombs in Japan.

Above: Celebrations continue into the early hours of the morning in Piccadilly Circus.

Opposite above: The Royal Family on the balcony at Buckingham Palace.

Opposite below: Crowds gather at Piccadilly Circus to celebrate the Japanese defeat a few days before Japan's official surrender.

Victory Parade

In September 1945, a huge Allied victory parade was held in Berlin to celebrate the 'victory of right over the black forces of aggression in the Far East'.

Above: British light tanks during the parade in Berlin.

Opposite: Almost one year on from the end of the war, members of the Royal Family assemble to watch a huge RAF fly-past on Victory Day 1946.

The Nuremburg Trials

After the war, many Nazi leaders were brought to trial at Nuremburg as war criminals. They appeared before the court in November 1945 and the trials were to last for several months. Of the 21 defendants, three were acquitted, seven received prison sentences ranging from ten years to life, and the remainder were sentenced to death, including Herman Goering. He escaped hanging, however, by committing suicide, swallowing a cyanide capsule which he had kept hidden throughout the trial. The executions of the others took place on 16th October 1946.

Above: The defendants listen to the summing-up.

Left: The verdicts are read out on 1st October 1946.

Opposite: An armoured car stands guard outside the Palace of Justice on the day before sentencing.

Above: Prisoners in the dock
during the Nuremburg trials.
Goering is at the far left.

Right: Rudolf Hess (left) and
Joachim von Ribbentrop
during a mealtime at the
Nuremburg courthouse.

The World's Biggest Conflict

When the largest conflict the world had ever known finally came to an end, it had claimed the lives of an estimated 55 million people, the majority of whom were civilians. Some 20 million Russians, 10 million Chinese and 6 million European Jews, who were never part of the 100 million mobilised to fight, are believed to have perished. Modern warfare had been characterised by the employment of advanced technologies, which had led to the deaths of civilians across the globe, and had culminated in the use of the atomic bomb, the threat from which continues to overshadow our existence to this day.

Above: On 16th June 1948 a ceremony took place in Cardiff as the remains of over 4,000 American soldiers, most killed during the D-Day landings, were loaded aboard the US *Lawrence Victory* bound for New York.